TAI CHI
HANDBOOK

TAI CHI
HANDBOOK
Exercise, Meditation, and Self-Defense

HERMAN KAUZ

A DOLPHIN BOOK
DOUBLEDAY
NEW YORK LONDON TORONTO SYDNEY AUCKLAND

A Dolphin Book

PUBLISHED BY DOUBLEDAY

a division of Bantam Doubleday Dell Publishing Group, Inc.
666 Fifth Avenue, New York, New York 10103

Dolphin, Doubleday, and the portrayal of two
dolphins are trademarks of Doubleday, a division of
Bantam Doubleday Dell Publishing Group, Inc.

Library of Congress Cataloging in Publication Data
Kauz, Herman.
    Tai chi handbook: exercise, meditation, and self-defense.
    1. T'ai chi ch'üan.   I. Title.
GV481.K38   796.8'159   73-10552
ISBN 0-385-09370-5

To my teacher Cheng, Man-ching

I wish to thank David Hayes for arranging for the taking of the photographs, acting as my partner in the photos demonstrating push-hands, and for typing the manuscript. Virginia Dwan and Steve Katz provided useful suggestions and help on the manuscript. Experiments in Art and Technology, Inc., which commissioned the photography for one of its cultural history projects, was kind enough to allow the photographs to be used in this book. I am grateful to Peter Moore, the photographer, for his work on the photographs. Finally, I am greatly indebted to Bonnie Crown for her efforts and support concerned with the manuscript's publication.

CONTENTS

INTRODUCTION

This country over the last few years has, with increasing frequency, seen the appearance of newspaper and magazine articles, as well as books, extolling the value for Western society of a centuries-old Chinese form of exercise and self-defense known as *tai chi*. *Tai chi* is usually translated as "grand ultimate." Some writers call it *tai chi chuan,* the *chuan* meaning "fist" or "boxing." We read that practicing tai chi prevents illness in the healthy, cures those who are ill of ailments ranging from arthritis to heart trouble, and makes possible the extension of life far beyond the traditional three score and ten. Viewed as self-defense, it is claimed that tai chi training enables a man to easily avoid an assailant's attack and without effort send him flying. In addition, some writers maintain that the duration of our daily practice need be neither long nor strenuous to achieve these results.

Statements such as the foregoing certainly make tai chi seem attractive to those of us who know we should do some form of exercise, or learn self-defense, but are unwilling or unable to work very hard for results. Some are too busy to devote a few hours a week to exercise, while others are unable to perform the strenuous activity called for by most exercise systems. Easy exercise of short duration which confers physical and mental benefits seems exactly what most of us need. However, the often unbounded enthusiasm of teachers and students for their particular art must not be permitted to cloud our vision. Before accepting the claims of the adherents of tai chi concerning its value, we should attempt to know more about this art. How accurate are the claims made for tai chi? Does practicing tai chi really prevent and cure illness? If tai chi does confer certain benefits, how much daily practice is necessary to gain them?

In connection with seeking answers to the foregoing questions, it may be interesting and instructive to briefly touch on a relevant aspect of Chinese culture. Scholars concerned with the Chinese language have pointed out that Chinese writers often exaggerate in order to strengthen their arguments. For example, a long beard on an old man is described by one writer as "gray hair, 3,000 feet long." Quantities or measurements of one sort or another are usually written in thousands, even though tens or perhaps hundreds would be more appropriate.

A related point concerns the ambiguity of the ideographs used to express ideas in written Chinese. A particular ideograph usually carries a number of meanings. Translations of ideas expressed by these ideographs into another language are often liable to error. This is especially so if the subject in question is esoteric. Sometimes there is no attempt at literal translation. The appearance or quality of some object may inspire the translator to change the original name. For instance, the preserved egg called in Chinese *pi-tan* (skin egg) is known in English as the hundred- or thousand-year-old egg. This egg is only about one hundred days old and has been preserved in lime and mud. This process causes the egg white to turn transparent brown and the yolk greenish black.[1] The English name might easily lead the unwary to believe that this egg is far older than it is.

Thus, because of the possibility of deliberate exaggeration and of error that may stem from translating statements written in Chinese into another language, it is usually advisable to regard apparently extravagant statements concerning esoteric subjects having their origin in China with a degree of skepticism. More specifically, to avoid disappointment, it is best to subject statements about tai chi's effectiveness in preventing or curing illness to the light of Western scientific method. This is not to hold that only Western science has all the answers in this area or that the health-care system practiced in the United States is in any sense perfect. However, if claims are made which seem to vary widely from our experience in this area, it would be sensible to submit such claims to rigorous examination.

The historical background of tai chi is somewhat obscure. It is difficult and overly optimistic to attempt to make definitive statements concerning events which occurred centuries ago and which were perhaps of interest to relatively few at the time. Nevertheless, tai chi appears to have its roots in systems of exercise and self-defense designed over the centuries to prevent illness of body and mind. Some of these movement systems were also used by sages and philosophers to enhance self-realization in themselves and in their students.

Some historians trace tai chi's origins to a man who watched a fight between

---

[1] *Joyce Chen Cook Book,* by Joyce Chen. J. B. Lippincott Co., Philadelphia and New York, 1962, pp. 157–58.

a serpent and a crane. The crane attacked the serpent repeatedly with stabs of its beak, but the snake, by shifting its body at the right moment, never allowed the crane to touch him. The interested viewer of this battle came up with the idea of a method of dealing with an attack that uses flexible maneuvers, correct timing, and sensitivity to avoid the opponent's offensive moves.

Others have suggested that tai chi grew out of a style of boxing, in existence for some centuries, which emphasized development of internal power and external flexibility and elasticity. Forms were usually practiced slowly and carefully in an attempt to develop sensitivity and heighten perception. Through the efforts of its originator, tai chi evolved, or was formed, as a complete system within this "soft" or "internal" boxing style.

Whatever its origins, its founder, and later tai chi theorists, tied it to certain philosophical concepts drawn from Taoism and, to a lesser extent, Confucianism. They took for its symbol the ancient Taoist diagram used to depict the principle of opposites, called *yin* and *yang* by the Chinese, connected in harmony. (See diagram.) These opposites represent the negative and positive aspects of the universe. Essentially, this symbol in tai chi illustrates the desire for avoiding extremes, for mental and physical balance, and for a method of living in harmony with the various overwhelmingly powerful forces in the world.

Taoism advocates other philosophical principles which seem relevant to tai chi. Ideas concerned with the yielding overcoming the non-yielding are interpreted by tai chi masters as using the opponent's strength to defeat him. The Taoist principle of *wu wei* (effortlessness or non-action) is considered in tai chi to mean using, when necessary, only that amount of force required to achieve an end. Overdoing is shunned. In the tai chi form, students are taught to use only that degree of strength necessary to perform a movement, thereby conserving energy and avoiding unnecessary tension.

The tai chi form, which students must learn first, is a method whereby a person can practice the maneuvers used in self-defense without the aid of a partner. Over the years, this form underwent change both in the number of movements included and in the way these movements were performed. The general principles of developing both sensitivity and the ability to free the body of tension, however, remained constant. The number of movements was few at first but gradually expanded to a few score. Some present-day systems of tai chi contain over one hundred movements. However, some of these movements are done more than once, and the actual number of basic positions is well under one hundred. The complete form in these systems takes 20 to 25 minutes. In recent times, efforts have been made to shorten the form. This attempt stems largely from an effort to reduce the amount of time necessary to learn the complete series of movements. It was thought that a reduction of this nature would permit a greater number of persons to learn the form.

The form presented in this book consists of sixty movements, some of which are repetitions. At the rate of attending classes once a week and practicing at home each day to fix the segment learned firmly in mind, it takes about five months to learn the complete form. Depending on the speed of performance, seven to ten minutes are required to do the form. In general, the sixty sequential, rhythmical movements are done slowly because speed tends to de-emphasize attention to the correct placement of feet and hands. Moving fast also reduces the ability to sense and maintain the proper co-ordination of hand and body movement with the shift of weight from one foot to the other.

Students of tai chi are attracted to it for reasons which range from a need for exercise to a search for spiritual enlightenment. Whatever our view of the possibilities in tai chi, we must do our best to be clear-minded and realistic about what it can do for us. Not every approach to such a study is ultimately beneficial. For example, some students are drawn to tai chi because of an interest in the exotic. Perhaps they are disaffected with their own culture and hope to find a more compatible philosophical climate in the culture of some other country. They often begin to study the philosophy and language of a culture that attracts them and sometimes seek to immerse themselves as far as possible in whatever elements of the foreign culture are available in their particular environment. Generally, these students tend to idealize the foreign culture. They are prone to be unquestioning in their acceptance of the worth and utility of ideas and practices said to be in vogue in that culture. Sometimes they go a step farther and become attracted by ways of behaving common to some past imagined golden age of the other culture. Often the people of the country in question have completely rejected the values held in the past because in practice these values lent themselves to corruption and misery on many levels.

Another aspect of this kind of behavior is to consider the teacher of the particular art they are studying as a kind of sage or, at least, as embodying the noblest characteristics of the culture they feel drawn to. They see him as knowing all about life and possessing wisdom to the same relative degree of superiority in relation to themselves as the expertise he displays in his art. His pronouncements on areas of life concerning which he may have limited knowledge are listened to with attention and willing acceptance. Unfortunately, this attitude detracts from a student's achieving any semblance of the Western ideal concerning social and political life which holds that a man must gather all available evidence, consider it carefully, come to a decision, and, if a vote is in order, have his voice counted as the equal of the next man's.

On the other hand, interest in another culture might stem from an attempt to gain the perspective necessary to better understand our own culture. We can all benefit by learning more about the world we live in. However, we are much more the product of the particular culture that we grew up in than we realize. If we study another civilization because we might wish to live in some other way, we overlook the fact that the way we think and feel and our modes of expressing ourselves are not the same as those of persons formed by another culture. The term "culture shock" denotes the adverse mental and emotional impact of another culture on persons attempting to live their lives in an alien environment. It relates to the inability to respond to the daily problems of life in a way characteristic of persons native to that environment. Culture shock refers to the negative psychological impact on us of situations in which we feel that a particular problem has simply not been handled in a way we know to be correct and right. Thus, it seems quite certain that in most cases we are only deluding ourselves when we feel that the ways of thinking and feeling common to people of another country would suit us better than those of our own.

Perhaps the healthiest way of dealing with products of another culture is to recognize ways in which they can improve our own. Any wholesale change in our culture to make it over into one that is like a foreign model, past or present, is clearly out of the question. However, "cultural borrowing," in which some foreign way of thinking or doing that seems to have relevance for a culture is incorporated into it, has long been characteristic of all cultures. The borrowed element fills some need and also usually undergoes change to allow it to better fit into its new home. This change often brings new life and vitality to the borrowed element as well as making it palatable to that part of the population repelled by the esoteric or put off by the exotic. The following chapters attempt to demonstrate that tai chi constitutes this kind of cultural borrowing and that its practice can enhance the quality of our lives.

TAI CHI
AS EXERCISE

Extravagant claims have been made for tai chi regarding its health-promoting and health-restoring qualities. If tai chi is considered as an exercise, what claims can legitimately be made for it?

In general, people who do some form of exercise on a regular basis (at least three times a week for one hour per period) have better circulation, better muscle tone, and fewer illnesses than people who do no exercise. In addition, those who exercise usually enjoy a feeling of physical and mental well-being. Most writers on fitness concern themselves with the effect of regular exercise on the heart and circulatory system. They generally share the conclusion that if we are to remain in good health, the heart must be given work beyond the minimal demands made on it by sedentary living. Recommended exercises are varied, including among others, jogging, swimming, tennis, golf, and skiing. Emphasis during the workout periods is on gradually giving the body more work to do until an optimum level of fitness is reached, measured by pulse rate before, and at stated intervals after, exercise. Certain exercises seem more suitable for some age groups than for others. Thus a milder form of exercise is usually recommended for older people, persons in poor health, or those who are recovering from an illness.

When considered strictly as a fitness-producing exercise, how does tai chi compare with an activity like jogging or swimming? The experience of students who have practiced tai chi regularly over a number of years is that their level of fitness has improved. They judged this level subjectively, usually noting an increased ability to climb stairs or to work longer periods without fatigue. Some who also jog for two or more miles felt that tai chi does not build endurance to the same degree as running. In their estimation, the latter activity calls for a greater expenditure of energy over a given time than does tai chi. Twenty minutes of jogging increases the pulse rate far above that reached in performing tai chi for a like amount of time. One breaks into a sweat after a few minutes of jogging, but in tai chi sweating is an indication that too much energy is being expended. Thus, when viewed simply from the standpoint of physical fitness, tai chi can be categorized as a mild form of exercise that promotes fitness and builds stamina, but to a lesser degree than do more strenuous forms like running or swimming.

Tai chi may, however, be an ideal way to exercise for many people who are interested in attaining and maintaining a reasonable degree of physical fitness and for whom a high level of fitness is unnecessary. Those who begin to practice tai chi soon realize it is not effortless. The tai chi form demands a considerable amount of work by the leg muscles because it is done with bent knees in a kind of quarter squat. Weight shifts from foot to foot as we do the form, but we do not stand fully erect until the form is completed. As we improve, we find we are able to sink lower in the form. This process gradually strengthens the legs and increases their muscle tone. Better leg development is beneficial to the health in a number of ways. Foremost among these, according to writers on cardiovascular fitness, is that firm, strong leg muscles help circulation. The well-known authority on heart disease, Dr. Paul Dudley White, has said:

> A . . . very important aid to the circulation, and incidentally to the heart, consists of the pumping action of the muscles of the extremities, particularly of the legs. The valves in the veins prevent the blood from going away from the heart when the veins are squeezed by the contracting muscles about them. Thus, the pull of gravity in the body's upright position is counteracted by good muscle tone and activity in the legs, and more blood is directed to the heart to be passed on, in turn, to the brain and other vital tissues.[1]

Because the tai chi form excludes extreme movements and emphasizes gradualness in learning, its practitioners avoid the pulled muscles and other injuries that sometimes accompany more strenuous activities. Students are not called upon to twist and turn in a way that might cause parts of the body to suffer strain. Instead, a feeling of restraint is encouraged and no movement is ever forced. Some sports and exercises couple maximum range of movement with maximum speed, a combination that can injure the body. A tennis

---

[1] *Fitness for the Whole Family,* edited by Paul Dudley White, M.D., and Curtis Mitchell. Doubleday & Company, Inc., Garden City, N.Y., 1964. Article is by Paul Dudley White, "A Doctor Looks at Fitness," p. 5.

or golf swing performed when we begin playing without a proper warm-up can cause pulled or torn muscles.

The possibility of such injury increases when exercise is left to weekends and is not done three or four times a week. Authorities on the subject are in accord that this is a dangerous practice because the body is not accustomed to the demands made on it and will react adversely instead of being helped. A milder form of exercise which can be done daily is much to be preferred to a more strenuous one performed infrequently. Tai chi, which can be practiced in one's living room and needs no special equipment, is well suited to daily exercise.

If people are to exercise regularly, month after month and year after year—a requirement that fitness experts consider important for continued good health—they must have an exercise that is interesting. Calisthenics become boring. Running laps around a track, or swimming from one end of a pool to another, often becomes mentally tiresome. Jogging over changing terrain is interesting for some, but weather conditions sometimes prohibit this form of exercise. Few activities can match the variety and interest of the tai chi form. The movements are based on self-defense techniques and are varied. Because attention must be given to balance and co-ordination, it is difficult to do the form automatically. Performing an exercise that absorbs our attention is important because it has been demonstrated that people generally derive less than optimum benefit from doing exercise they consider uninteresting or boring.

In addition to its value in developing physical fitness, practicing tai chi as an exercise also develops in us the ability to use our body in a more efficient way. By "efficient" is meant, first of all, that the legs become strong enough to fully do the job of supporting and transporting the body as we stand, walk, and run. When the legs are weak there is a tendency for muscles of the upper body to be used to compensate and, as a result, to become tense. Balance often is impaired under these circumstances. Secondly, our bodies work more efficiently when we learn to relax because we conserve energy. We tire more quickly if we expend energy unnecessarily by tensing muscles which are not needed to perform a movement. Emphasis while doing the form is on using only the minimum of strength needed to accomplish an action. Finally, we can learn to use our body fully in whatever we are doing. For example, we should open a door with our whole body and not just our arm. Except for work done while sitting, the large muscles of the body, and especially the legs, should be brought into play in everything we do. Tai chi can teach us to move in this more efficient way.

Learning to relax contributes to a more efficient use of the body, but it confers benefits beyond this. Relaxation receives major emphasis in tai chi. As we do the form, muscles unnecessary to a particular action are kept loose and free of tension. Shoulders are not raised or tightened, the chest is not thrown out or forward, breathing becomes deeper, and the stomach is permitted to move in and out with each breath. Finally, the hands and wrists are never tensed. The over-all effect aimed at, however, is not slackness or collapse, but an alert relaxation which in an instant can respond to some external threat. Unfortunately for those who want quick results, the attainment of this relaxed state is not a matter of a few weeks. Our fast-paced, often hectic lives produce a degree of tension in our bodies that most of us are unaware of. It takes months and even years for some students to release this tension. It is a gradual process, but it produces a feeling of calm and well-being that is new and welcome.

Other forms of exercise also help relax their adherents. The more strenuous sports release tension through a rapid expenditure of energy that results in a relaxed body when the game or exercise is over. To some extent, performing tai chi also relieves built-up tension through action. However, although release of tension in this manner is beneficial for the health, its effects are often only temporary. After resting from our workout, we often find ourselves becoming tense again as we return to our jobs or to other tension-producing activities. The lesson learned in tai chi is that we must stay relaxed and as free from tension as possible, not only when we are practicing tai chi, but at other times as well. This emphasis on relaxation is shared by few forms of exercise and contributes in large part to tai chi's attractiveness and usefulness for modern urban society.

Most people who are aware of their physical tension also notice that they are mentally tense. Often mental and emotional tension manifests itself physically. An increasingly important search for many city dwellers is for a measure of tranquillity in their lives. Of late, researchers on the effect of stress on people's health have found that this phenomenon is one of the chief causes of heart disease and other major illnesses. The findings are that persons who share certain personality traits—the hard-driving, highly competitive men— are more susceptible to stress than individuals who take an easygoing attitude toward life. If one is a stress-prone individual, what can be done to reduce stress or counter its injurious effects? Although unanimous agreement is absent, many scientists seeking ways to reduce the harmful effect of stress on people have recommended exercise. This prescription squares with the author's experience over many years of learning and teaching martial arts. For example, students who practice karate have remarked enthusiastically on the marked feeling of tension release they achieved when performing their punches or kicks. Karate is, however, an activity which calls for a high degree of physical conditioning. It can satisfy and benefit only a relative few of the many who need this kind of help. By contrast, tai chi can be practiced by almost everyone.

Some students, whose primary purpose in studying tai chi is to relax and to release their tension, report they have been helped to remain cool in the face of a verbal or psychological attack, thereby avoiding the negative effects of stress. Others have commented on their new ability to work and play at a slower pace as a result of their involvement with tai chi. Such a change, however, especially for those most in need of functioning in a more restrained manner, does not come in a short time. Progress in this direction is slow and often requires years of training. This is understandable in cases where these persons continue in the same job or where other environmental factors which contribute to their tensions remain unchanged.

It may be profitable to examine tai chi's contribution to health from still another standpoint. In speaking of the way the human body works, doctors of Chinese medicine often refer to a life force, or vital energy, called *chi* which flows through the body on specific pathways. This vital energy can be tapped at some seven hundred points on the body where the pathways come to the surface. These points are used in acupuncture to correct an imbalance in the energy flow which has adversely affected the functioning of some internal organ.

Western scientists have attempted through dissection to find the pathways of this vital energy but have had no success. Yet Western doctors have seen acupuncturists cure apparently incurable diseases. Acupuncture seems to work, even though it is not yet clear how it works. Consequently, many European doctors have begun using acupuncture in their treatments over the last twenty years. The visit of American newsmen to China in 1972 saw an upsurge of interest in this country in the medical possibilities of acupuncture. Especially emphasized was the use of acupuncture as an anesthetic in major and minor surgery.

Dissection of cadavers, however, may not be the only way to determine whether the vital energy and its pathways actually exist. This vital energy apparently ceases to flow after death. In 1939 in Krasnodar, Russia, an electrician named Semyon Davidovich Kirlian discovered a method of photography, using high-frequency electrical fields, that can record on film the energy coming from the human body and from plants.[2] Some years later, Dr. Mikhail Kuzmich Gaikin, a Leningrad surgeon, read about Kirlian's work. He was reminded of the explanation for acupuncture that he had heard

---

[2] *Psychic Discoveries behind the Iron Curtain,* by Sheila Ostrander and Lynn Schroeder. Prentice-Hall, Inc., Englewood Cliffs, N.J., 1970, p. 199.

19

from Chinese doctors during his army service in China. He went to see Kirlian. As Gaikin and Kirlian looked at the photographs of a human body under high-frequency electrical fields they found:

> . . . the spots where lights flared most brilliantly appeared to match the acupuncture points the Chinese had mapped out thousands of years ago! Gaikin was excited. Just possibly the Kirlian discovery might give the first scientific confirmation of this five-thousand-year-old system of medicine. Maybe there was also a relation between the pathways of swimming light the Kirlians saw and the pathways of Vital Energy described by the ancient Chinese.[3]

After studying the Kirlian process, Dr. Gaikin, in collaboration with an engineer, Vladislov Mikalevsky, developed an electronic device called the "tobiscope" that locates the points on the body into which the acupuncture needles are inserted. These points are less than a millimeter wide and traditionally difficult to pinpoint accurately. The tobiscope finds the position of the acupuncture points within a tenth of a millimeter.[4]

The results of this kind of research point to the possibility that the *chi* written of by ancient teachers of tai chi may be more than an indulgence in poetry or an effort to embue their art with magic. It may be totally in keeping with reality to think that, when we are doing the tai chi form in a correct, relaxed way, we are opening the pathways along which this vital energy flows. Opening these pathways may have the effect of correcting imbalances in this energy flow with consequent benefits to our health. The evidence already in certainly suggests that it would not be amiss to do tai chi with the expectation of insuring or aiding the proper functioning of our internal organs. Moreover, tai chi as an exercise may then be ultimately far more beneficial for our health than its non-strenuous appearance would indicate.

Another reason for making this statement is related to a previous point concerning gradualness and restraint in the use of the body while learning and doing tai chi. The body is not forced to perform beyond comfortable limits. These limits are gradually extended as strength and flexibility increase with daily practice. Breathing is not forced or tampered with as in some systems of exercise and meditation. Instead the body is permitted to take in the amount of air it needs on the assumption that it is the wisest judge of its requirements. If we notice the changes in our breathing as we do the form, we become aware that after a few minutes of practice our breathing becomes deeper and slower. This happens naturally and without direction by our conscious mind. In the same way, doing the form in as relaxed a way as possible,

---

[3] *Ibid,* p. 223.

[4] *Ibid,* p. 225.

and with correct posture, permits our body to function freely and naturally, instead of being forced into the cramped and twisted contortions or the hyperextensions necessary in some sports and exercises.

Of course, the conscious mind plays its role, too. We must decide whether or not we need some form of exercise in the first place, and we must choose that form of exercise which will be ultimately most beneficial. The author's experience, however, indicates that the above-stated respectful approach to the body's functioning is the one which will serve us best as we go from youth into middle and old age.

Students usually ask how often and for how long a period they must practice to realize the health benefits outlined in this chapter. Remember that the body cannot store exercise. In order to remain healthy, we must maintain a certain level of activity throughout our life. Muscles must be used if they are to retain their strength and their tone. In the author's judgment, a daily period of exercise totaling 30 minutes is of optimum benefit. This period should come at a time of day when we are not rushed. Students find that setting aside some time in the evening in which to do the form and to unwind is most practical. Others prefer to do the form once or twice in the morning, soon after rising, and again twice at night, shortly before going to bed. Still others find it beneficial to devote their lunch hour to practicing tai chi. Whatever pattern we find most suitable should become habit just as much as brushing our teeth, or washing up. Exercising should be considered an essential part of our life—essential because it provides the strength and health that enables us to travel the longest distance possible along our chosen path.

TAI CHI
AS MEDITATION

Exercising, or learning to relax physically, is not the only way for the tension-ridden to find peace and tranquillity. Some have turned to alcohol and others to drugs to slow their racing mental and emotional engines, only to find that these methods of relieving strain result in harmful side effects. A smaller percentage has tried various forms of meditation. Tai chi, in addition to conferring the health benefits related to exercise, can be thought of as moving meditation. Many who have done sitting meditation (*zazen*) in an effort to achieve tranquillity have been strongly impressed by the usefulness of tai chi for this purpose. For some, the flowing, slowly unfolding form of tai chi is more suitable for meditation than sitting motionless in one place. Still others consider a moving meditation highly satisfying philosophically because they believe everything in the universe is constantly in motion and they can harmonize best with the universe through a meditation that also moves. Those who are attracted by Chinese philosophy (Taoism and Confucianism) see in tai chi a physical expression of the principles expounded in these systems of thought. Whatever a student's reason for meditating, whether stemming from a desire for relief from mental tension or a longing for some form of spiritual enlightenment, engaging in it can have a number of mind-quieting and mind-expanding results.

Meditating can help us to attain a state of mind in which our thoughts are not constantly jumping from past events to hoped-for or feared events in the future. We can slowly learn to focus attention on each present moment. These moments are, after all, our real experiences of life and should be savored to the full instead of being diluted by thoughts of past and future. The tai chi form serves ideally for this purpose, because, if it is to be correctly performed, we must give it our full attention. Extraneous thoughts and ideas intrude as we are doing the form, but these should not be entertained. The mind must immediately return to focus completely on the correct performance of the form. Gradually we become able to concentrate fully on the form for longer and longer periods, without becoming distracted by problems and thoughts which had previously caught and held our attention.

The lessons learned in this kind of activity carry over into the rest of our day. We become increasingly capable of fully living each moment instead of living in the past or future. In addition, after a practice period we often return to our troubles with a new perspective. Somehow a problem's proportions seem reduced. What had earlier seemed threatening, and perhaps overwhelming, becomes capable of solution. We are no longer completely at the mercy of an overactive imagination that prepares us physically and mentally for events that usually fail to happen, or at least not with the dire results we have projected.

Practicing tai chi as meditation can provide that period of quiet and calm necessary for all of us if we are to maintain our mental equilibrium under the trying conditions of today's world. It is no waste of time to spend a part of each day in an activity which relaxes us mentally and physically, allows us to pull our scattered thoughts together, and removes us from the necessity of interaction with others. Time spent in this way renews us and enables us to face our responsibilities with additional strength. Furthermore, over a period of time we can develop the kind of concerted, direct, relaxed approach to a difficult job that often results in its completion in relatively short order.

Related to this kind of mental and emotional integration is the concept of gathering or centering energy. The fast pace at which we carry on our lives causes us to expend energy at a greater rate than is wise, in directions which contribute little to our long-term goals. We often have a feeling of having wasted our physical and mental strength. We are tired out with not enough to show for our efforts. If we could gain additional control over our energy expenditure, we could learn to use energy less wastefully. As explained above, by learning to perform the movements in the form with the very minimum of effort, training in tai chi promotes the physical conservation of energy. But beyond that, tai chi as a meditative art teaches a mental and emotional energy conservation and control that enables us to focus our energy more fully in directions we decide are really productive.

Tai chi as meditation can help us to be more open and receptive to new ideas and to other people than we have been. By relieving the tension, and the often accompanying hardness in our mental and emotional makeup, we can begin to interact with others in a more satisfying way. People usually respond to an emotionally relaxed and receptive person in a friendly manner. If we refrain from forcing our ideas on others and are willing to listen to theirs, our personal relationships might be much more fruitful. In addition, because a tense, closed mind prevents us from sampling anything new, a more relaxed mental attitude could expose us to a wider range of experience and add additional dimensions to our lives.

Finally, a realistic view of the world is possible only as our awareness grows of the many unexamined ideas and prejudices through which we filter our impressions of life. Most of us experience extreme difficulty in changing our particular way of relating to the world even if we begin to suspect that our method prevents us from seeing what is really there. A change of this nature is often resisted because it makes us different from our friends and from society in general. However, for those who must see and experience the world as it really is, the kind of mental relaxing and "letting go" possible in tai chi is essential.

Psychologists and others concerned with mental and spiritual health maintain that a rigid attitude of mind stems from fear of life—of people, of new experiences, and of what the future may hold. Moreover, they suggest that a negative and fearful attitude toward life brings negative results. For example, if we believe we are going to be sick, before too long we achieve the result that our mind is seeking. Many thinkers on this subject hold that the mind plays a leading role in health, general well-being, and success in life. If we wish positive results in our lives, we must begin to think positively.

To carry this theme a step further, some suggest it is both realistic and beneficial to believe that we are part of a greater force or spirit which works through us. We are not alone. If we could but open ourselves to the working of this spiritual force, the range of life's possibilities would broaden. To work for, and gradually to achieve, a relaxed state of mind in tai chi serves ideally to prepare the ground for this kind of spiritual opening up.

It must be understood, however, that in using meditation to realize the desirable results mentioned above, progress comes slowly. Everyone who does tai chi as meditation makes some progress toward realizing his goals, but the degree of progress varies both with the nature of the goal and with the mental, emotional, and physical makeup of the particular person involved. Additional factors to consider are the frequency and duration of practice, as well as the degree of concentration achieved during practice. Thus, in measuring the distance we have advanced toward our objectives, we should not be impatient or overly dissatisfied with our progress. We usually get from our practice what we put into it. If we begin our study with certain physical or mental handicaps, these factors may inhibit or retard progress. Such restrictions may consist only of weak legs, a tendency toward laziness, or an inability to concentrate. Handicaps of this nature can, however, be offset and overcome by devoting additional time to practice.

TAI CHI
AS SELF-DEFENSE

Some people are drawn to tai chi because they want to learn to defend themselves from physical attack. They may have seen or heard about a skilled exponent of this art effortlessly sending an assailant flying away to crash against a wall or some other object. This kind of magic certainly has its fascination.

Not all students share this fascination, however, judging from the substantial number who do not move on to "push-hands," as the self-defense aspect of the art is known. In the normal progression, the form is first thoroughly learned and then students are expected to begin push-hands. As they are taught the form, they begin to realize that it is based on self-defense movements. Sometimes their teacher makes the point that a more complete understanding of the mechanics and dynamics of the form does not come until they have done push-hands for a time. Despite these hints, many students are content to do only the form. Perhaps a brief and perforce slightly oversimplified description of push-hands is in order at this point.

Push-hands is a kind of sparring in which partners stand facing one another and, without moving their feet, attempt to unbalance each other using the very minimum of strength. All movements are usually performed slowly. If the movements are too quick it is difficult for both attacker and defender to sense what is actually happening. When an attack comes, we must learn to sense the amount and direction of the opponent's force, neutralize it by not presenting a surface for him to push or strike against, and at the same time strike him or cause him to lose his balance. The emphasis is on developing the ability to interpret the opponent's attack and, by shifting one's body, cause him to miss his target. Missing the target, and expecting resistance where there is none, usually results to some degree in loss of balance. We must capitalize on this mistake and the resultant weakness by instantly counterattacking. In practice, the counterattack actually develops while the opponent is going off target. If properly done, only a minimum of force is necessary to send him flying a number of feet away.

In the author's experience, students fail to engage in the practice of push-hands for reasons which range from the seemingly obvious ("I just can't make it at that time") to those that the student refuses to acknowledge even to himself. (Perhaps physical contact with another person is upsetting.) Thus, to begin with the apparently straightforward, some students expect a relatively quick flowering of self-defense ability. The expectation is that a particular way of dealing with an opponent's attack can be quickly learned from the teacher's demonstration and will then become part of a self-defense arsenal to be used whenever that same attack is encountered. However, training in tai chi proceeds along entirely different lines. The intention is to develop an over-all sensitivity as well as the kind of efficient use of the body that can generate tremendous force in an instant. Once attained, these attributes enable the student to neutralize and effectively counter any form of attack. Moreover, this training confers the ability to respond immediately to changes in the opponent's attack. Even practitioners of those martial arts which rely heavily on strength and speed realize that they also must have the ability to instantly change direction or focus. The opponent's reaction to an offensive, or defensive, move cannot be taken for granted. His reaction must be recognized, evaluated, and appropriately dealt with—all within a split second.

At any rate, when this hoped-for and expected self-defense ability does not begin to materialize over the period of a month or two, some students lose interest. They may feel that they can never become sufficiently proficient in push-hands to be able to use it to defend themselves. Perhaps accustomed to quick results in other areas of learning or development, they find it impossible to understand why their attempt to learn push-hands in a few months meets with failure. If these students believe strongly that they require some form of self-defense, they may be drawn to one of the many schools that foster the illusion of self-defense in ten easy lessons.

Another category of students who are repelled by push-hands includes those who experience anxiety when placed in what appears to be a competitive situation or in one that calls for a direct confrontation with another person. They may fear, or be unwilling to recognize, their aggressive and perhaps hostile impulses. Consequently, they try to avoid situations in which they might encounter aspects of their personality they wish to deny.

Still others resent, or are unable to bear, being in the position of appearing mentally dull or stupid. This situation occurs frequently in push-hands when a beginner is paired with a more experienced student. Try as he might, the beginner is usually unable to neutralize his partner's attack and finds himself repeatedly pushed off balance. Those accustomed to solving abstract intellectual problems rather quickly fail to understand why the same result is not forthcoming in push-hands.

Avoiding the study of push-hands is, in most cases, unfortunate because students who fail to continue their training after learning the form are often those who could benefit immensely from this practice. Were they to attempt push-hands they could gain knowledge not easily available elsewhere about efficient body movement and about self-defense. Of even greater importance, they would learn more about themselves.

At the outset, as stated above, a clearer perception of the movements in the form results from practicing push-hands. Dealing with another person gives us a much better understanding of how we must use our bodies instead of just our arms in a particular movement. Thus after many unsuccessful attempts to push the opponent or to neutralize his attack with only our arms and shoulders, we learn through experience that our whole body must be utilized. We begin to comprehend what is meant by having our feet planted, or rooted, firmly in the ground. We realize the importance of hip and waist flexibility in neutralizing an attack and at the same time returning force to the opponent. As we do push-hands we notice that every action is a co-ordinated one, with all parts of the body simultaneously in play. We understand the need for a low center of gravity and a balanced stance. We apprehend directly the negative effect of tension and the positive value of a relaxed body. All these ways of using the body and of relating to the environment are precisely those we are attempting to implant in the tai chi form. It is then obvious that experience in push-hands enables us more easily to sense and fulfill the requirements of the form.

Push-hands clearly illustrates the detrimental effect of unnecessary tension in any physical effort. If our body is tense as we attempt to push the opponent off balance, he can more easily sense our intention and can usually neutralize the attack. We lose flexibility and with it the possibility of adjusting our attack to a change in his balance or in the position of his body. If the situation is reversed and we attempt to neutralize an attack with a tense body, the result is also usually failure. Tension produces an inability to clearly perceive the direction and amount of force in an attack. In addition, even if the opponent is for some reason off target, we must first relax in order to make an appropriate response.

It is difficult, when doing the tai chi form, to fully realize the amount of tension in our body. Physical tension becomes much more noticeable in pushing hands. Not only are we better able to sense the presence of tension in ourselves, but, in addition, the opponent also helps make us aware of it, either by telling us of it or by successfully attacking us. Had tension not been present, he would have had no surface to push against and his attack would have failed. Although the opponent is useful in this respect, he is also for most of us an additional complication. Often he constitutes a threat in the form of a competitor whom we must overcome. This way of thinking usually increases our tension. A better way to relate to our opponent is to consider him just as necessary to our development as we are to his. Both of us are really attempting to perfect ourselves and are helping one another to do this. This kind of attitude often reduces or removes the negative presence of competition that can easily enter push-hands. Avoiding a competitive approach to push-hands helps greatly to reduce tension.

Physical tension is usually the outward manifestation of some kind of inner unease. Another attribute of practicing push-hands is the opportunity for self-knowledge. As we grow more relaxed while doing push-hands, we become more aware of our reactions to others. If we did not know them already, we begin to learn the answers to such questions as: Do we tense up and become rigid if someone attacks us in a strong, determined way? What happens in us when we sense hostility from our opponent? Do we consciously, or perhaps unconsciously, express hostility? Do we want to win at all costs? Answers to these questions can contribute greatly to a better understanding of ourselves. This is a necessary first step in the direction of achieving a more desirable way of living.

As one example of this kind of development, many students report they have become able to apply the lessons learned in push-hands to other aspects of their lives. In their interaction with others they feel better equipped to neutralize much of the hostility and aggression they encounter. Of course, this training takes place primarily on the physical level in push-hands. Nevertheless, students seem able to extend the general way of thinking, characteristic of neutralizing the opponent's strength in push-hands, to the broader area of non-physical, interpersonal relations.

From the foregoing, it seems obvious that in push-hands we can learn a great deal about ourselves. We are also afforded the opportunity to know a great deal about the character of our opponents. Moreover, the knowledge is very direct because it is non-verbal. To some this method might seem a step backward to an earlier stage in man's development. However, words and conversation are often used by people to disguise their real intentions and feelings. They often do this unconsciously or, if consciously, because they feel that it is dangerous to let others see them as they really are. They believe words can shield and protect them. If we attach a great deal of importance to verbal communication, it is only when we have closer or more intimate relations with others that we begin to see them more clearly. Interaction with others in an activity like push-hands lets us know a number of truths about our opponents quickly and directly. The words we usually use do not get in the way.

How useful is tai chi as a defensive art? Many who watch the slow movements peculiar to push-hands fail to see its value as self-defense. Based on their past experience with martial arts, they expect to see an exhibition of techniques performed with great strength and speed. Tai chi, however, depends less on strength and speed than do other martial arts. The major emphasis is on fostering the ability to interpret the direction and force of the opponent's attack and to neutralize this attack by moving the body just enough to cause him to miss his target and lose his balance. The instant of disequilibrium must be used to counterattack. In training, little attention is given to developing physical strength or generating great speed. Sensitivity and flexibility are stressed. Because of the emphasis on the acquirement of sensitivity in tai chi, those who practice it can continue to improve over the years. Our ability to refine our sensitivity does not diminish with advancing age. In contrast, the often heavy reliance on strength and speed, characteristic of many other martial arts, becomes increasingly difficult as we grow older.

It should be obvious that gaining the kind of ability which can enable us to overcome a physically superior opponent is the work of many years. A year or two spent doing push-hands once or twice a week barely gets beneath the surface. Faster progress, of course, comes with more concentrated practice (daily, for an hour or more), but this kind of dedication is out of reach for most of us. Those who want to learn to defend themselves relatively quickly would be advised to spend two or three years studying karate. Martial arts, which rely heavily for success on power and speed, can be learned much more quickly than tai chi. However, if we are to undertake this kind of training, youth and some degree of athletic ability are very helpful. Furthermore, to achieve real proficiency in an art like karate also takes many years, and here too there is ultimately a decreasing reliance on strength and speed.

A realistic look at the situation seems in order here. How often have the majority of us had to physically defend ourselves from attack? We generally do our utmost to avoid trouble and stay clear of violence. Many of us may have felt threatened at one time or another and would have been more secure in the knowledge that had a physical attack actually materialized we should have been able to cope with it. Achieving some skill in tai chi can provide this confidence. However, the most important benefit that tai chi push-hands training can give is the ability to remain calm in the face of the threat of physical violence. The ability to remain cool under these circumstances enables us to determine the course of action best suited to the occasion. If it should happen that we are physically attacked, we must defend ourselves, but in very few situations need this extreme occur. If we are sensitive and alert—a condition that tai chi training brings about—we should be able to notice impending danger and take appropriate action in time to avoid a possibly disastrous confrontation. Seeing danger early enough to avoid it, or to prepare the means to neutralize it, is the secret of survival. Self-defense is, therefore, much more than a physical ability to overcome assailants. The physical side of it is employed only when every other possibility has failed.

A final word is in order concerning the practice of push-hands in tai chi. Not too much will be said of the mechanics and the intricacies of push-hands. There is really no way of grasping this art intellectually. It cannot be learned by hearing or reading about it. Here, as in so many other endeavors, there is no substitute for personal experience. We must find a competent teacher, place ourselves in his hands, and then practice diligently in the manner he prescribes. As our sensitivity grows and we become more skillful, we will begin to know for ourselves the efficacy of tai chi and its vast potential as self-defense.

TAI CHI
FORM

General Considerations

As you do the tai chi form, remember the following points. Performing each movement with these considerations in mind will be difficult at first, but with continuous practice, the recommended ways of holding the body and moving will become automatic and feel natural.

1. *Keep the body perpendicular to the ground.*

Maintain a straight line from the bottom of your spine through the top of your head. Imagine you are a marionette suspended from a point at the top of your head. Under these circumstances, leaning in any direction is impossible. Moreover, if your body is perpendicular to the ground, good balance is more easily maintained. Thus, your weight can go directly into the center of each foot. This condition is partly responsible for the strong stance, or rootedness, characteristic of those who have attained some degree of skill in tai chi.

2. *Breathe naturally.*

Make no particular attempt to co-ordinate breathing with movement. Avoid forcing abdominal breathing. After a few minutes of doing the form, breathing becomes deeper without conscious effort. As your familiarity with the form increases, some attention might profitably be given to exhaling when performing an attacking movement. However, emphasis on breathing in the early stages of learning the form tends to introduce an unnecessary complication into the situation.

3. *Eliminate all unnecessary tension from the body.*

Tension impedes the flow of energy generated in the body. Use only enough strength to complete the required movement. Avoid tensing any muscle. Imagine the arms are raised by a kind of levitation and that the muscles are not involved in the process. As you do the form, keep the chest relaxed and the shoulders down. Avoid raising the elbows unnecessarily as you perform the various movements. Permit your abdomen to swell and contract naturally with each breath.

4. *Maintain a low center of gravity.*

Except for a few positions, keep the knees bent in about a one-quarter squat. Avoid straightening the knee as weight shifts from one leg to the other. In general, the head should neither rise above nor fall below a set horizontal plane as one position changes to the next.

5. *Think of the lower abdomen as the body's center.*

The lower abdomen and the area around it (hips and waist) must be involved in every movement. If this part of the body is not correctly utilized, the effectiveness of techniques will be considerably reduced.

6. *Maintain one continuous speed.*

Avoid speeding up or slowing down. In general, do the form slowly and carefully without stopping and without increasing the speed at points that seem familiar or easy. Reflecting nature, the form is constantly in motion. Usually, as one movement develops to its prescribed maximum extent, it changes, without stopping, into a movement in the opposite direction.

7. *Co-ordinate arm and hand movements with body movements.*

In general, arms and hands begin to move the instant the body starts its movement. Such body movement usually occurs when weight shifts from one leg to the other. The moment body movement ends, arm and hand movement ends.

8. *Think of the air as possessing the tangibility of water.*

Move your hands in the air as if you can feel it. Doing the form is sometimes likened to swimming in air.

9. *Remain alert.*

Although the form can be considered a moving meditation, avoid thinking of it as a withdrawal from life or merely a looking inward. Be aware of your surroundings to the extent that your mind registers everything around you. Become sensitive to external as well as internal happenings.

10. *Concentrate fully on performing each movement with the mind as well as the body.*

Perform each movement to the utmost of your capabilities. For example, if you are pushing, direct your mind outward in the direction of the push. At the same time, give full attention to foot and hand positioning, proper balance, timing, and the release of all unnecessary tension. Avoid letting the mind wander.

Recurring Positions and Movements

1. Throughout the tai chi form, one position recurs frequently. This position will be termed the "70-30 stance." The name is chosen because in this stance 70 per cent of the weight is considered to be on the front foot. However, it is difficult to accurately determine the percentage of weight carried on each foot. Thus, the major requirement is that more weight is carried by the forward than by the back foot. Correctly done, this stance must meet the following requirements in whichever direction you face:

A. Head and eyes—head up, facing straight ahead. Eyes gazing forward levelly.

B. Forward foot—bears 70 per cent of the weight (or at least a greater percentage than the back foot) and points directly forward.

C. Back foot—points diagonally at 45 degrees to the forward foot.

D. Relation of feet to one another—if the forward foot is brought straight back along the direction it points and the toe of the back foot is turned inward until the feet are even and parallel, a foot should be under each shoulder. In assuming the stance, if the back leg is properly bent (one-quarter squat) and the heel of the front foot is set down empty of weight, the length between the feet will be correct.

E. Knees—both bent. Leading surface of forward knee about an inch behind toes. Thigh of back leg is perpendicular to the ground.

F. Hips and shoulders—squarely forward. In whatever direction you face, insure that one hip or shoulder does not precede the other.

G. Elbows and shoulders—as relaxed as possible and lowered as much as possible while still meeting the requirements of the position.

H. Hands and arms—positions vary.

2. In general, keep the nose and navel lined up vertically. Thus, when the body turns, the head also turns. Eyes look straight ahead, but not to the exclusion of noticing developments around you. Peripheral vision permits awareness of movements within a 180-degree range. Alertness is an important aspect of the tai chi form.

3. Become aware of the difference between "full" and "empty." In tai chi the leg bearing the greater part of the body weight, or generating the greater thrust, is considered "full." For maximum efficiency and power in a movement, the arm on the opposite side of the body from the full leg strikes the blow or delivers the force. Thus, if 70 per cent of the body weight is on the left leg, the right hand delivers the major attack. Because the form is done without a partner, it is difficult to observe the effect of this way of using the body. However, the reason for doing the form with the idea of full and empty in mind will become clear and pay dividends when you advance to "push-hands."

A related point concerns the hand which is not full. Avoid allowing this hand to merely dangle as if you had forgotten it for the moment. The empty hand must retain its sensitivity because the situation to which you are responding may change in an instant, causing a sudden switch in the function of the hands. Moreover, were an opponent to attempt to grasp the empty hand, it must respond in an appropriate manner. A correct and timely response is impossible if you have momentarily forgotten the hand.

4. Wrists, elbows, and knees always remain at least slightly bent. The wrists should maintain a slight convex curve so that where the hand is open this curve extends from the forearm into the hand and into the fingers. Elbows and knees never lock out completely even in those positions or movements where the opportunity to do this exists.

Starting Position

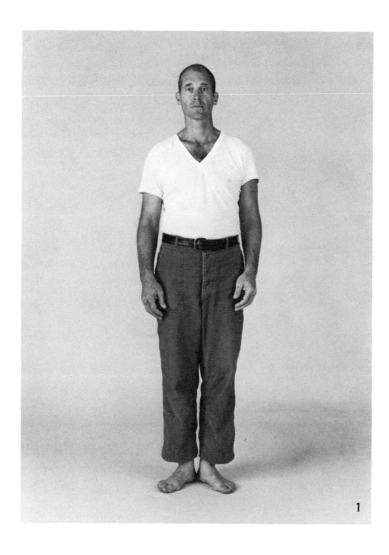

Stand erect, facing forward with the heels together, toes pointing out so the feet form a V. (To provide a point of beginning for directional changes, consider the direction you are facing as north.) Arms and hands hang loosely at the sides. Head is up, and the eyes look straight ahead. Shoulders are relaxed. Chest is relaxed and not held up or forced out. Stomach is not tensed or pulled in but is permitted to move naturally in and out with each breath. The mouth is closed with the tongue against the roof of the mouth and the tip of the tongue behind the upper front teeth (Figure 1).

1. Preparation

A.   Shift all of your weight to your right foot, bending the right knee slightly. At the same time, raise your left heel, move your elbows slightly away from your sides, and rotate your hands until the backs of your hands face forward (Figure 2).

B.   Take a step about 12 inches to the left (west) with your left foot, and position the foot so that it points straight ahead. Shift your weight to your left foot (Figure 3).

C.   Straighten your right foot by turning your toe in until the foot points straight ahead and is parallel with your left.

D.   Shift your weight to the right until it is evenly distributed between both feet. At this point, feet are parallel, with one foot under each shoulder. The toes of one foot are even with those of the other. Knees are very slightly bent. Elbows are slightly separated from your sides and the backs of your hands face forward (Figure 4).

2. *Beginning*

A.   As if your wrists are being drawn upward by invisible strings, allow your arms to rise in front of you to a point about shoulder height. One hand is in front of each shoulder. Keep the hands dangling loosely as you raise the arms. Elbows are slightly bent and allowed to hang down. Avoid raising the shoulders as the arms come up (Figure 5).

B.   When the wrists reach shoulder height, the palms and then the fingers straighten until they are parallel with the ground (Figure 6).

C.   Slowly withdraw the hands toward your shoulders, again permitting the palms and fingers to hang loosely.

D.   Move the elbows past your sides and allow the hands to sink downward. The heels of your hands lead the way down as the hands return to their starting position (Figure 7).

37

3. Grasp Bird's Tail (Ward Off with Left Hand)

8 9 10

A. Shift most of your weight to your left foot, bending the left knee some-what more, and turn your right toe directly to the right (east). As your foot turns, rotate the hips, shoulders, and head as far as possible in the same direction (east). Simultaneously, raise your right hand, palm down, in the center of your body to the level of your armpit and bring your left hand, palm up, to a point in front of your lower abdomen. Position the hands as if they are holding a ball of air between them (Figure 8).

B. Shift all of your weight to your right foot, allowing your left heel to leave the ground. As your weight moves to your right foot, bend the right knee until you are in a one-quarter squat. Throughout this shift maintain your hand and body position (Figure 9).

C. Just before your weight is completely on your right foot, begin to turn your body to the left (counterclockwise). Then step straight out (north) with your left foot, placing the heel on the ground first. Insure that your left foot moves straight out in the direction in which it was pointing and that it is not drawn toward the right foot (Figure 10).

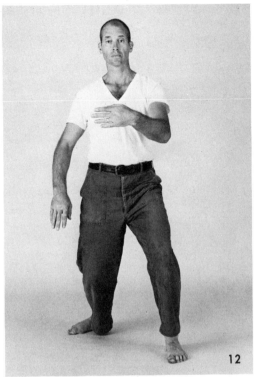

D. Transfer 70 per cent of your weight to your left foot, continue to rotate your body to the left, and raise your left hand in front of your body, palm facing you, to a point slightly above the solar plexus. Simultaneously, lower your right hand, palm down and to the rear, to a point just to the right of your right thigh (Figure 11).

E. Just before weight transfer and hand movement conclude, rotate your body until your hips and shoulders face directly north. In addition, turn your right toe inward 45 degrees (northeast) (Figure 12).

Position Check

1. Feet, legs, body, and head fulfill requirements of 70-30 position. (See p. 33.) Direction is north.

2. Left hand—in center of body about two inches above solar plexus, with palm facing body.

3. Right hand—just to right of right thigh, with back of hand facing forward. Elbow slightly bent.

4. Grasp Bird's Tail (Ward Off with Right Hand)

13

14

A. Continue to shift your weight to your left foot, allowing your right heel to rise. Simultaneously, turn your left palm down and bring your right hand forward, palm up, in front of your lower abdomen. Thus, palms again face one another as if you were holding a large ball of air between them (Figure 13).

B. When weight is almost 100 per cent on your left foot, begin to turn your body to the right (clockwise). With all of your weight on the left foot, lift your right foot and place the heel where the toe was. Be sure the right foot points directly east (Figure 14).

C. Shift 70 per cent of your weight to your right foot. At the same time, your right hand must rise toward shoulder level at the center of your body, the palm facing you. The left hand remains in its position and moves with the body as you turn (Figure 15).

D. As weight transfer and hand movement conclude, rotate your body until your hips and shoulders face directly east. While rotating the body, turn your left toe inward 45 degrees (northeast) (Figure 16).

Position Check

1. Feet, legs, body, and head fulfill requirements of 70-30 position. (See p. 33.) Direction is east.

2. Right hand—in center of body, shoulder high, with palm facing body. Distance from body about 16 inches.

3. Left hand—fingertips about three inches behind right palm. Palm faces down and slightly outward. Fingers point toward right wrist.

5. Grasp Bird's Tail (Rollback and Press)

A.   Without shifting weight or moving your arms, rotate your hips, shoulders, and head 30 degrees to the right (clockwise) (Figure 17).

B.   Shift most of your weight to your left foot. Simultaneously, lower your left hand, palm up, to a point near your right elbow. At the same time, bring the right hand and forearm closer to your body (Figure 18). Co-ordinate your hand movements with the shift of weight so that when your body stops moving your hands are in the required position.

C.   Turn your body to the left (counterclockwise), allowing your left hand to travel down to the rear and then up to a point about level with your ear. Permit your right hand and arm to move with your body as it turns (Figure 19).

17

18

D. Reverse the direction of your turn and shift your weight forward until it is 70 per cent on your right foot. At the same time, move your left hand forward until the palm makes light contact with the wrist and heel of the right hand (Figure 20).

Position Check

1. As in position 4, feet, legs, body, and head fulfill requirements of 70-30 position. (See p. 33.) Direction is east.

2. Right hand—same as in Position 4, except that it is a few inches closer to the body.

3. Left hand—palm lightly touching wrist and heel of right hand. Insure that back of left wrist is slightly convex or rounded and does not form an angle.

6. Grasp Bird's Tail (Push)

A. Begin to shift your weight to your left foot. The instant your body begins to move, separate your hands and bring them and your forearms closer to your body. Turn your right hand so the palm faces foward. When most of your weight has moved to your left foot, both hands are in front of the shoulders, with the palms turned out toward the front (east) (Figure 21).

B. Shift your weight forward again until your right foot bears 70 per cent of your weight. At the same time, your hands and forearms move forward in a push. Co-ordinate the forward movement of the hands and forearms with that of the body, to insure that all motion ends at the same instant (Figure 22).

Position Check

The only difference from Positions 4 and 5 is in the hands. Both hands are in front of the shoulders, with palms facing outward. Wrists are shoulder height and the back of each wrist is slightly convex. Forearms are a little more vertical than horizontal and elbows are bent about 90 degrees.

21

22

7. Single Whip

A. Transfer your weight to your left foot and allow your hands to drop until they and your forearms are almost parallel to the ground. Move away from your hands and allow your elbows to straighten somewhat more (Figure 23).

B. When almost all of your weight is on your left foot, begin to turn your body and your right toe to the left (counterclockwise). Turn your body as far as it can go toward the left (even as far as northwest). Arms and head turn as your body turns (Figure 24). To perform this movement correctly, arms and hands must follow the rotation of the body and point straight toward the direction you are facing. In the tai chi form, the nose and navel usually remain lined up vertically, making necessary a turn of the head as the body turns.

C. Transfer your weight to your right foot. As the weight shifts, rotate your body slightly to the right (clockwise) and draw your hands in next to your right side. The right hand, as it withdraws, forms a kind of hook, with the fingertips all lightly touching and the knuckles lower than the wrist. The left hand moves, palm up, to a position near your right hip and just below the right hand. Note that the right elbow is lower than the right wrist and that the hands are not touching (Figure 25).

23

24

25

D. With all of your weight on your right foot, begin to turn your body toward the left (counterclockwise) until you face northwest. As you turn, pivot on your left toe and allow your right hand in its bent (hook) position to move diagonally toward the northeast. The hand rises slightly until the upper surface of the right wrist is at shoulder height (Figure 26).

E. Take a big step to the left and slightly forward and place your heel, empty of weight, on the ground. Position the left foot in accordance with the requirements for the front foot of the 70-30 position (Figure 27). Shift 70 per cent of your weight to your left foot and simultaneously bring your left hand forward, palm facing you (Figure 28). When almost 70 per cent of your weight has shifted, rotate your body and head counterclockwise until you face directly west, turn your right toe inward 45 degrees (northwest), and turn your left palm outward. The right hand moves very little as your

body turns. Its movement terminates at a point slightly behind your right hip (Figure 29). This action stretches and helps relax the shoulder joint.

Position Check

1.   Feet, legs, body, and head fulfill requirements of the 70-30 position. (See p. 33.) Direction is west.

2.   Left hand—in front of left shoulder, palm facing outward, wrist and top of shoulder along the same horizontal plane. Elbow bent 90 degrees.

3.   Right hand—fingertips held lightly together, knuckles lower than wrist. Upper margin of wrist shoulder high. Elbow slightly bent and relaxed. Hand a little behind right hip.

8. Lift Hands (Right)

A.   Begin to shift your weight to your left foot, allowing the heel of your right foot to rise. At the same time, release the "hook" formed by your right hand, and turn it and the left hand so that the palms face one another.

B.   Just before 100 per cent of your weight reaches your left foot, begin to rotate your body toward the right (clockwise) (Figure 30). Looking north, but with your body facing northwest, bring your hands and arms toward each other until the left palm faces and is about six inches away from the right elbow.

C.   Simultaneously with the hand movements, move your right foot a few inches to the left in front of you so that if it were brought straight back, it would just miss hitting your left heel. Set the right foot down, bearing no weight, with only the heel touching the ground (Figure 31).

30

Position Check

1. Head and eyes—face north.

2. Left foot—points west, bearing 100 per cent of the weight.

3. Right foot—points north, bearing no weight, with only the heel touching the ground. If brought straight back, it would just avoid hitting the heel of the left foot.

4. Knees—both bent, the left more than the right.

5. Hips and shoulders—facing northwest.

6. Right hand—palm facing west. Hand and arm pointing north in line with right leg. Angle at elbow about 120 degrees. Hand slightly below shoulder height.

7. Left hand—palm facing right elbow and about six inches away from it. Elbow close to left side and bent about 90 degrees. Outer surface of left and right wrists slightly curved (convex).

9. Shoulder Strike

A.   Lower your hands toward your pelvic area, the right palm directly facing your groin and the left facing your left thigh. Simultaneously, bring your right foot straight back and place the toe, without weight, near the heel of your left foot (Figure 32).

B.   Step directly forward again with your right foot, place the heel on the ground (Figure 33), and as the rest of the foot is set down, shift 70 per cent of your weight to it. As your body moves forward, raise your left hand, palm down, to the level of your right elbow. Avoid letting the fingertips of the left hand extend beyond the right elbow.

C.   Just before your weight is fully 70 per cent on your right foot, rotate your body very slightly counterclockwise (Figure 34). This final movement is designed to bring the right shoulder into contact with an opponent's chest.

Position Check

1. Head and eyes—face north.

2. Right foot—points north, bearing 70 per cent of the weight. If brought straight back, it would just avoid contact with the heel of the left foot.

3. Left foot—points west.

4. Knees—both bent. Insure that leading surface of right knee does not extend beyond toes of right foot.

5. Hips and shoulders—instead of facing directly northwest as in Figure 33, they now face more to the west.

6. Right hand—palm facing groin area, elbow slightly bent.

7. Left hand—palm down at level of right elbow. Avoid letting fingertips extend beyond right elbow.

10. Stork Spreads Wings

A.   Begin to shift your weight forward until all of it rests on your right foot. Simultaneously, start to raise your right hand and rotate it until the palm faces outward near your right temple. As the right hand rises, the left lowers and moves, palm down and to the rear, toward a point just to the left of your left thigh. As your weight shifts to your right foot, turn your body to the left (counterclockwise) until the hips and shoulders face almost directly west (Figure 35).

B.   As the movement concludes, raise the body slightly, and move the left foot about 12 inches diagonally (northwest) to the right. Set the foot down pointing directly west, without weight and with only the toe touching. Insure that both hands and your left foot reach their terminal positions at the same instant (Figure 36).

35

Position Check

1. Head and eyes—face west.

2. Right foot—points north, bearing 100 per cent of the weight.

3. Left foot—points west, only the toe touching the ground. If brought straight back, the foot would just miss hitting the heel of the right foot.

4. Knees—both slightly bent. Right knee bent more than left.

5. Hips and shoulders—face almost due west.

6. Right hand—about four inches from right temple, palm facing out. Elbow on level with jaw.

7. Left hand—just to left of left thigh, palm facing down and to rear.

36

11. *Brush Knee and Twist Step (Left)*

A.   Lower your body slightly and drop your right hand straight down. As the hand lowers, revolve it, allowing its edge to lead in its downward path and ending with the palm facing up (Figure 37).

B.   Rotate your body clockwise until your hips and shoulders face almost directly north. Simultaneously, bring your right hand back and up to a point level with your ear, and move the left hand, with fingers pointing down and palm facing the body, in a circle toward your right side (Figure 38).

C.   Just before your hands end their move to the right, take a step about 10 or 12 inches to the left and slightly forward (west) with your left foot. Set the heel down first. As the left heel touches the ground, the right hand reaches the top of its swing and turns over with the wrist relaxed and the fingers pointing ahead (west) (Figure 39).

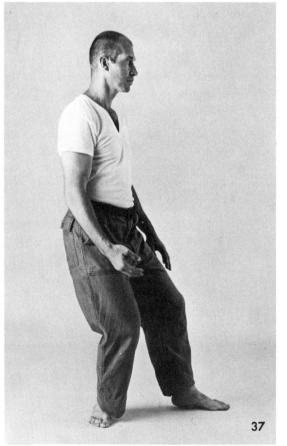

37

38

D.   Shift your weight 70 per cent to your left foot and rotate your body to the left (counterclockwise) until you face directly west. At the same time, bring your right hand forward to a point in front of your right shoulder and move your left hand, fingers down and palm facing your body, across your groin area, stopping just to the left of your left thigh. As your body and hands end their movement, turn your right toe inward 45 degrees (Figure 40).

Position Check

1.   Feet, legs, body, and head fulfill requirements of 70-30 position. (See p. 33.) Direction is west.

2.   Right hand—in front of right shoulder, palm facing out (west), wrist and top of shoulder along same horizontal plane. Elbow bent 90 degrees.

3.   Left hand—just to left of left thigh. Palm faces down and to rear. Elbow slightly bent.

39

40

12. Lift Hands (Left)

A. Without moving your hands, leaning forward, or raising the body, transfer all your weight to your left foot. To keep from elevating the body, bend the left knee a bit more than in the 70-30 position (Figure 41). Raise your right foot slightly off the ground and set it down again, toe touching first. The direction in which it points is slightly more northerly than in the 70-30 position.

B. Shift your weight to your right foot. The instant your weight begins to shift, raise your left hand and bring it across toward the right (north). Lower your right hand until your right palm faces, and is six inches away from, your left elbow (Figure 42).

C. The moment your left foot is free to move, shift it about ten inches to the right (north) and set it down, bearing no weight, with just the heel touching. Co-ordinate the movement of the left foot with that of the hands and the body so that all action concludes at the same instant (Figure 43).

41

42

Position Check

1. Head and eyes—face west.

2. Right foot—points 30 degrees west of north, bearing 100 per cent of the weight.

3. Left foot—points west, bearing no weight, just the heel touching the floor. If brought straight back, it would just avoid hitting the right heel.

4. Knees—both bent, the right more than the left.

5. Hips and shoulders—face slightly to the north of west.

6. Left hand—palm faces north. Hand and arm point west in line with left leg. Angle at elbow about 120 degrees. Hand slightly below shoulder height.

7. Right hand—palm faces left elbow at a distance of about six inches. Elbow bent 90 degrees and close to right side. Outer surface of left and right wrists slightly curved (convex).

43

13. Brush Knee and Twist Step (Left)

Rotate your body toward the right (clockwise) and allow your hands to move with your body, circling downward toward your right thigh and then rising (Figure 44). At this point, follow directions beginning with B in Position 11. Note that the right toe turns in only slightly as the movement ends, instead of the 45 degrees called for (Figures 45, 46).

46

14. *Deflect Downward, Parry, and Punch*

A.   Shift your weight to your right foot. At the same time, turn your body as far toward the southwest as possible. As weight comes off your left foot and as your body turns, turn your left toe toward the southwest also. Simultaneously with the weight shift and body turn, lower your right hand until the palm faces, and is a few inches away from, your groin (Figure 47).

B.   Move forward and transfer all of your weight to your left foot. As your body moves ahead, form a loose fist with your right hand. Co-ordinate the formation of the fist with your forward movement so that both end at the same instant (Figure 48).

C.   Take a small step straight forward with your right foot and set it down, heel first, pointing diagonally toward the northwest (Figure 49). Transfer your weight to your right foot, allowing your hands to lag behind you and circle upward (Figure 50).

D.   Raise your hands higher and then bring them forward, the left hand moving forward beside your head in a downward chop to a point slightly left of the body's center, a little below shoulder height. The right hand makes a circle in front of you, at solar plexus height, and drops, knuckles down, at the side of your right thigh. As your hands move forward, step ahead with

47

48

49

your left foot and set it down, heel first, pointing west. Because the punch requires the 70-30 stance, insure that your foot placement provides enough length and width between the feet. As you step forward, rotate your body to your right (clockwise) so that it faces slightly north of west. Co-ordinate the movement of the hands and left foot so that all three reach their terminal positions at the same instant (Figure 51).

E.   Shift your weight forward until 70 per cent is on your left foot. As you move ahead, raise your right fist and revolve it counterclockwise until it is vertical. Insure that your right elbow stays close to your side as you raise your fist. Complete the movement by rotating your body counterclockwise until your hips and shoulders face directly west. Use this rotation to complete your right-hand punch. The punch ends at solar plexus height in the center of your body and about six inches forward of the left hand (Figure 52).

Position Check

1.   Feet, legs, body, and head fulfill requirements of 70-30 position. (See p. 33.) Direction is west.

2.   Left hand—slightly to left of body's center, fingertips a little below shoulder height. Edge of hand faces down. Elbow bent about 90 degrees.

3.   Right hand—in center of body at height of solar plexus. Fist is loosely held, is vertical, and extends six inches beyond left hand. Elbow close to right side.

50   51   52

15. *Apparent Closure*

53

54

A. Rotate your body slightly to the left (counterclockwise), opening your fist and extending your right hand toward the left (southwest) (Figure 53). Shift most of your weight back to your right foot and withdraw your right hand to a point in front of your chest, palm facing you. As your right hand withdraws, lower your left hand slightly, turn the palm up, and bring it in toward your chest. The right forearm, as it pulls back, moves across your left wrist (Figure 54). When both hands face your body they form an X, with the left hand outside the right (Figure 55).

B. Shift your weight forward until 70 per cent is again on your left foot. Simultaneously, separate your hands and turn the palms outward in a restrained push (Figure 56).

55   56

Position Check

1. Feet, legs, body, and head fulfill requirements of 70-30 position. (See p. 33.) Direction is west.

2. Left and right hands—in front of shoulders with palms facing outward. Wrists are level with the tops of your shoulders. Forearms are more vertical than horizontal. Elbows bent 90 degrees.

16. Cross Hands

A. Transfer your weight to your right foot. At the same time, rotate your body to the right (clockwise) and turn the toe of your left foot toward the right until it points directly north (Figure 57).

B. Shift your weight to your left foot. Allow your right hand to move outward and downward as you shift to the left. Simultaneously, let your left hand move outward and downward toward the left and continue to turn your body until your hips and shoulders face directly north. As your body completes its turn, pivot on the toe of your right foot until the foot points due north (Figure 58).

C. When all of your weight is on your left foot, draw the right foot straight back and set it down parallel to the left, one foot under each shoulder with the toes even (one foot not ahead of the other). At this moment, your hands will have completed their downward course and are turned so the palms face your body. Transfer half of your weight to your right foot. As the weight shifts, raise your hands in front of you to form an X, slightly below shoulder level, about 12 inches in front of the body. The left hand is closer to you than the right. At the conclusion of this position, weight is equal between the feet (Figure 59).

Position Check

1. Head and eyes—face north.

2. Feet—parallel, pointing north, one foot under each shoulder. Insure that toe of one foot is not ahead (farther north) of the other. Weight evenly distributed between the feet.

3. Knees—bent in a one-quarter squat.

4. Hips and shoulders—face directly ahead (north).

5. Hands—crossed about 12 inches in front of body slightly below shoulder height. Left hand is closer to body than right.

57

58

59

17. Carry Tiger to Mountain

60

61

A.   Shift your weight to your left foot. As weight begins to transfer, the right palm turns down and the left palm up, with the backs of the hands touching. Hands drop together toward the left thigh and the body begins to rotate toward the right (clockwise) (Figure 60).

B.   Circle the left hand upward to the left and slightly behind you until it reaches ear level where it turns palm down, fingers pointing in the direction you face. Simultaneously, take a long step straight to the rear with your right foot, point the toe southeast, and set the heel down without weight. The heel of your right foot sets down and your left hand reaches the top of its circle at the same instant (Figure 61).

C.   Shift your weight until it is 70 per cent on your right foot. As the weight moves forward, turn your body until you face southeast, bring your left hand forward, palm facing out, to a point ahead of your left shoulder. Simultane-

62

ously, move the right hand across the groin area, palm toward you and fingers pointing down, from the left to the right thigh. As the position concludes, turn your right hand palm up next to your right thigh and rotate the left toe inward 90 degrees (Figure 62).

Position Check

1. Feet, legs, body, and head fulfill requirements of 70-30 position. (See p. 33.) Direction is southeast.

2. Left hand—in front of left shoulder, palm facing out (southwest), wrist and top of shoulder along same horizontal plane. Elbow bent 90 degrees.

3. Right hand—just to outside of right thigh, palm up, elbow slightly bent.

18. Grasp Bird's Tail (Rollback and Press)

This movement repeats Position 5. Direction, however, is southeast instead of east. To arrive at the point which coincides with the instructions for Position 5, transfer your weight to your left foot. Simultaneously with the shift of weight, raise your right hand and lower your left. When your weight has moved to the left foot, your left hand is palm up near your right elbow and your right hand about shoulder height, palm facing to the left (Figure 63). Continue by following the instructions for Position 5, beginning at 5C (Figures 64, 65).

63

64

65

19. *Grasp Bird's Tail (Push)*

This movement repeats Position 6. Direction is southeast instead of east (Figures 66, 67).

66

6.

20. Single Whip

68

69

72

This movement repeats Position 7. Final direction is northwest instead of west (Figures 68, 69, 70, 71, 72, 73, 74).

70

71

73

74

21. Fist under Elbow

A.   Shift all of your weight to your right foot. At the same time, release the "hook" formed by your right hand and rotate the hand clockwise a one-quarter turn until the palm faces the left hand.

B.   Step to the left with your left foot and set it down heel first, pointing west. Position the foot so that if it were withdrawn in the direction it points, it would just avoid hitting the heel of your right foot (Figure 75). Transfer all of your weight to your left foot.

C.   Step diagonally to your right (northwest) with your right foot and set the whole foot down, pointing northwest. The right toe is in line with the back of the left heel (Figure 76). Transfer all of your weight to your right foot. As weight shifts, rotate your body counterclockwise and pivot on your left toe until your body faces southwest. As your body turns, rotate your left hand clockwise one-quarter turn until the palm faces outward to the rear (Figure 77).

D.   Your right hand circles with your body rotation until the hand points due west. Permit your left hand to move around behind your left hip. At this point, reverse your body's rotation to clockwise and bring the left hand forward and up, fingers leading, in front of your face. Simultaneously, form a

75

76

loose fist with your right hand, bring it in toward you, and place it directly below the left elbow. Just before your body completes its rotation and faces directly west, shift your left foot a few inches diagonally to the right and set it down without weight, pointing west, with only the heel touching the ground. Insure that all parts of your body stop moving at the same instant (Figure 78).

Position Check

1. Head and eyes—face west.

2. Right foot—points northwest, bearing 100 per cent of the weight.

3. Left foot—points west, only the heel touching the ground. If the foot were withdrawn along the direction it points, it would just avoid contact with the heel of the right foot.

4. Knees—right knee bent in a one-quarter squat. Left knee slightly bent.

5. Hips and shoulders—face west.

6. Left hand—in front of face, fingertips about eye level, edge of hand facing west. Forearm almost vertical and back of wrist slightly curved (convex).

7. Right hand—in a loose fist, held vertically, with the upper margin of the fist directly beneath the left elbow, but not touching.

77

78

22. Step Back and Repulse Monkey (Right)

A. Rotate your body to the right (clockwise) until it faces northwest. As you turn, open your right hand, lower it toward your right thigh and then raise it in a circle to the right rear, up to the level of your ear. Simultaneously, extend your left hand and arm farther forward (west), slightly below shoulder level, but do not fully straighten your elbow.

B. As your right hand reaches the top of its circle, level with your ear, flip it over so the palm faces down and the fingers point forward (west). The moment the right hand turns over, rotate the left counterclockwise so its palm faces up. Turn the hands together. At the same time, take a step to the left rear with your left foot, and set the toe down, without weight, in line with the back of your right foot. The left toe touches the ground just as your hands turn over (Figure 79). Insure that the left foot points straight ahead (west) as the rest of the foot makes contact with the ground.

C. Rotate your body toward the left (counterclockwise) until it faces west. At the same time, shift all of your weight to your left foot, bring your right hand forward, palm facing outward, to a point in front of your right shoulder, and lower your left hand to a point beside your left thigh, palm facing up. When enough weight has left your right foot, turn the toe inward until it points in the same direction (west) as the left foot (Figure 80).

Position Check

1. Head and eyes—face west.

2. Right foot—points west, bearing no weight.

3. Left foot—points west, bearing 100 per cent of your weight. If the right foot were drawn straight back, even with the left, one foot would be under each shoulder.

4. Knees—left knee bent in a one-quarter squat. Right knee slightly bent.

5. Hips and shoulders—face west.

6. Right hand—in front of right shoulder, palm facing outward (west), wrist and top of shoulder along same horizontal plane, elbow bent 90 degrees.

7. Left hand—beside left thigh, palm facing up, elbow slightly bent.

79

80

23. Step Back and Repulse Monkey (Left)

A.   Continue to rotate your body counterclockwise until it faces southwest. As you turn, raise your left hand in a circle to your left rear until it reaches ear level. Simultaneously, extend your right hand and arm farther forward (west), slightly below shoulder level, but avoid straightening your elbow completely.

B.   As your left hand reaches the top of its circle on a level with your ear, flip it over so the palm faces down and the fingers point forward (west). The moment the left hand turns over, rotate the right clockwise so its palm faces up. The hands turn over together. At the same time, take a step straight back with your right foot and set the toe down, without weight, in line with the back of your left foot. The right toe touches the ground just as your hands turn over (Figure 81). Insure that the right foot points straight ahead (west) as the rest of your sole makes contact with the ground.

C.   Rotate your body clockwise until it faces west. At the same time, shift your weight 100 per cent to your right foot, bring your left hand forward, palm facing outward, to a point in front of your left shoulder, and lower your right hand to a point beside your right thigh, palm facing up (Figure 82).

Position Check

1.   Head and eyes—face west.

2.   Left foot—points west, bearing no weight.

3.   Right foot—points west, bearing all of your weight. If the left foot were drawn straight back, even with the right, one foot would be under each shoulder.

4.   Knees—right knee bent in a one-quarter squat. Left knee slightly bent.

5.   Hips and shoulders—face west.

6.   Left hand—in front of left shoulder, palm facing outward (west), wrist and top of shoulder along same horizontal plane, elbow bent 90 degrees.

7.   Right hand—beside right thigh, palm facing up, elbow slightly bent.

76

81

82

24. *Step Back and Repulse Monkey (Right)*

Follow instructions for Position 22. The fact that the hands begin their movement from a different position should cause no difficulty. It is also unnecessary to turn the right toe inward at the conclusion of the position, because it already points west (Figures 83, 84).

83

84

25. Diagonal Flying

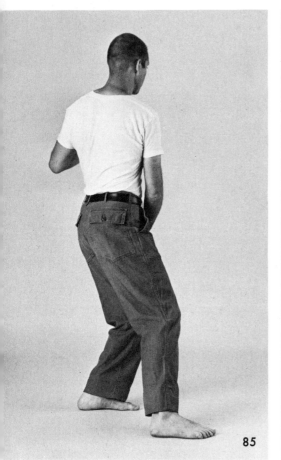

85

86

A. Continue to rotate your body counterclockwise until it faces southwest. As you turn, raise your left hand in a circle to a point near and slightly below your left shoulder and turn it over so the palm faces down. At the same time, lower your right hand and bring it, palm up, to a point just below your left hip. Palms face one another as if you were gently holding a large ball of air between them (Figure 85).

B. Rotate your body clockwise and take a long step to your right rear (northeast) with your right foot. Set the heel down first, pointing the foot northeast (Figure 86). Shift 70 per cent of your weight to the right foot. As weight shifts, raise your right hand, palm up, to a point level with your neck, fingers pointing northeast. Simultaneously, lower your left hand to a point to the left of your left thigh, palm facing the rear. As your body finishes its turn

87

and your hands assume their positions, turn your left toe inward 90 degrees until it points north (Figure 87).

Position Check

1. Feet, legs, body, and head fulfill requirements of 70-30 position. (See p. 33.) Direction is northeast.

2. Right hand—in line with right leg, fingers pointing northeast, palm up at level of neck, elbow slightly bent.

3. Left hand—about 12 inches to the left of the left thigh, palm facing the rear, elbow slightly bent.

26. Wave Hands Like Clouds (Right)

A. Shift all of your weight to your right foot, allowing your left heel to rise. Simultaneously, bring your right hand in toward your right side at about armpit level, revolving the hand as it withdraws until the palm faces down. At the same time, move your left hand under your right, palm up, at the level of your lower abdomen. Hands again hold a ball of air between them (Figure 88).

B. Take a short step forward with your left foot in the direction (north) the foot points. Step only far enough to insure that the toes of both feet are even when your right foot straightens and becomes parallel with the left (Figure 89). Begin to shift your weight to your left foot. As weight shifts, lower your right hand to the level of your lower abdomen and raise your left to a point slightly above the solar plexus. As your hands move, revolve them so the palms face your body at a distance of twelve inches (Figure 90).

C. Begin to rotate your body counterclockwise. As you turn, your hands move in a circle in front of your body toward your left side. In addition, the right toe turns 45 degrees inward until it points directly north and is parallel to the left. When your hands pass the middle of your body, weight is about equal between the two feet (Figure 91). Continue to shift your weight until it is 100 per cent on the left foot, and rotate your body until it faces northwest.

88

89

90

D.   As your weight shift and body rotation conclude, your hands will have reached your left side and turned so the left hand is palm down at armpit level and the right hand palm up at lower abdomen level. Palms face one another as if holding a ball of air (Figure 92). Finish the movement by taking a small step to the left with your right foot. Place the foot so it is parallel with your left, toes even, with feet shoulder width apart. Place no weight on the right foot (Figure 93).

Position Check

1.   Head and eyes—face northwest.

2.   Feet—point north and are parallel with toes even. Feet are shoulder width apart. Left foot carries 100 per cent of the weight.

3.   Knees—bent in a one-quarter squat.

4.   Hips and shoulders—face northwest.

5.   Left hand—at left side, armpit level, with palm facing down.

6.   Right hand—at left side, lower abdomen level, with palm facing up. Hands appear to hold a large ball of air.

91

92

93

27. *Wave Hands Like Clouds (Left)*

94
95

A. Begin to shift your weight to your right foot. As weight shifts, lower your left hand to the level of your lower abdomen and raise your right to a point slightly above the solar plexus. As your hands move, revolve them so the palms face your body at a distance of 12 inches (Figure 94).

B. Begin to rotate your body clockwise. As you turn, your hands move in a circle in front of your body toward your right side. When your hands pass the middle of your body, weight is about equal between the two feet (Figure 95). Continue to shift your weight until it is 100 per cent on the right foot and to rotate your body until it faces northeast.

C. As your weight shift and body rotation conclude, your hands will have reached your right side and turned so the right hand is palm down at armpit level and the left hand palm up at lower abdomen level. Palms face one another as if holding a ball of air (Figure 96). Finish the movement by taking a small step to the left with your left foot. Place the foot so it is parallel with

the right, toes even, with not quite double shoulder width separating the feet. Place no weight on the left foot (Figure 97).

Position Check

1. Head and eyes—face northeast.

2. Feet—point north and are parallel with toes even. Not quite double shoulder width separates the feet. Right foot carries 100 per cent of the weight.

3. Knees—bent in a one-quarter squat.

4. Hips and shoulders—face northeast.

5. Right hand—at right side, armpit level, with palm facing down.

6. Left hand—at right side, lower abdomen level, with palm facing up.

28. Wave Hands Like Clouds (Right)

Follow the instructions for Position 26, beginning with the sentence in paragraph B: "Begin to shift your weight to your left foot." Ignore that part of 26C which concerns turning the right toe inward. Feet remain parallel throughout the movement. In addition, as the movement concludes, the right foot remains where it is and does not move toward the left (Figures 98, 99, 100).

98

99

100

29. Single Whip

Step straight ahead (north) with your right foot, placing the heel on the ground first and pointing the foot north (Figure 101). Shift all of your weight to your right foot, allowing your left heel to leave the ground. At the same time, extend your right hand toward the north at shoulder level, forming a "hook" with the hand as it moves outward. Simultaneously, lower your left hand and extend it slightly beyond your right side, palm up (Figure 102). Follow the instructions for Position 7, beginning at 7E. Note that in the present situation the left foot need only be set down heel first, close to its present location, in order to be correctly positioned (Figures 103, 104, 105).

103

104

105

30. Snake Creeps Down

106

Rotate your body to the right (clockwise) until you face northwest. At the same time, turn your right toe 45 degrees to the right (north), and revolve your left hand clockwise until it faces the body (Figure 106). Shift most of your weight to your right foot and bend your right knee until you are in a deep squat. As your body begins to drop, turn your left toe inward 45 degrees and lower your left hand to the inside of your left thigh, fingers pointing down toward the knee and the palm facing away from the thigh (Figure 107).

Just before the right leg is fully bent, turn your left toe 90 degrees to the left (southwest) and, as your body continues to drop, thrust your left hand down along the inside of your left leg toward your ankle (Figure 108).

Throughout this movement, retain a slight bend in the left knee and maintain the position of your right "hook" hand. Also, as much as possible, keep your body perpendicular to the ground.

31. *Golden Cock Stands on One Leg (Right)*

109

110

A.   Shift your weight to your left foot and begin to rise. Simultaneously, raise your left hand, fingers leading and palm vertical, to a point slightly above and forward of your left shoulder (Figure 109). Rotate your body to the left (counterclockwise) until you face west. At the same time, turn your right toe inward 45 degrees until it points northwest, and rotate your left hand clockwise until the palm faces out (Figure 110).

B.   The moment 100 per cent of your weight reaches your left foot, draw your right foot (forward) and, releasing its "hook," bring your right hand in toward the front of your right hip (Figure 111). Continue these movements by raising your right knee in front of you to solar plexus level and thrusting upward with your right hand, fingers leading, until the right forearm extends upward vertically above the right knee. Simultaneously, lower the left hand, palm down, to a point just to the left of your left thigh. Avoid bending forward at the waist as you raise your right knee (Figure 112).

Position Check

1. Head and eyes—face west.

2. Left foot—points southwest, bearing 100 per cent of the weight. Left knee bent in a one-quarter squat.

3. Right foot—right knee in center of body, raised to level of solar plexus. Lower leg extends downward vertically. Foot and ankle are relaxed with toes pointing down.

4. Hips and shoulders—face west.

5. Right hand—forearm and hand extend vertically above right knee in center of body. Elbow about two inches above knee. Palm faces left (south) and fingers point upward. Back of wrist slightly curved (convex).

6. Left hand—slightly to left of left thigh, palm facing down and to rear. Elbow slightly bent.

32. Golden Cock Stands on One Leg (Left)

113

Lower your right foot diagonally to your right rear and place it on the ground, toe first, pointing 45 degrees to the right (northwest). Shift your weight to your right foot. As weight shifts, lower your right hand, palm facing down, toward your right thigh and begin to raise your left hand (Figure 113). As soon as you can raise your left foot, bring it up until your knee is in the center of your body at solar plexus height. As your knee comes up, thrust up-

114

ward with your left hand, fingers leading. Insure that your right and left hands reach their terminal positions at the same instant. As in Position 31, avoid bending forward at the waist as your knee comes up (Figure 114).

Check the final position of the various parts of your body against those of Position 31. Remember that, in the present position, actions are performed by the opposite hand or foot from that in the previous position.

33. Separate Right Foot

A. Lower your left foot diagonally to your left rear and place it on the ground, toe first, foot pointing southwest. Begin to shift your weight to your left foot. As weight shifts, bring your left hand down until the forearm is parallel with the ground and rotate the hand so the palm begins to face up. At the same time, rotate your body slightly to the left (counterclockwise), and raise your right hand, palm down, fingertips passing near your left elbow (Figure 115).

B. As weight continues to shift to your left foot, rotate your body in the opposite direction (clockwise). Simultaneously, continue to move your right hand, but now it circles outward diagonally toward the right (northwest). With 100 per cent of your weight on your left foot, the right hand is slightly below shoulder height, palm down, and elbow bent to form an angle somewhat greater than 90 degrees. The left hand is palm up just below and to the left of the right elbow. Head and eyes face diagonally right (northwest) and hips and shoulders face as much in that direction as possible, without any part of the body feeling undue strain (Figure 116).

C. Turn your body to the left (counterclockwise) until you face southwest. Simultaneously, lower your hands and then raise them in a circle beyond your left side and shoulder. As your body turns and hands move, turn your right toe inward 90 degrees to the left (Figure 117).

D. Rotate your body to the right (clockwise). At the same time, bring your hands forward to form an X in front of, and about eight inches from, your chest, slightly below shoulder height, left hand closer to your chest and above the right wrist. As part of your body rotation, turn your right heel inward until the foot points northwest, leaving just the toe touching the ground (Figure 118).

E. Just as your body completes its clockwise rotation and faces west, raise your right foot in a kick to the northwest, aimed at an imaginary opponent's knee. Simultaneously, rotate your hands to turn the palms outward and separate the hands, extending the right toward the northwest and the left toward your left side. Fingers of both hands point up. The right hand is in line with the right leg, and the left hand is to the left and slightly forward of your left shoulder (Figure 119).

Position Check

1. Head and eyes—face northwest in direction of kick.

2. Left foot—points southwest, bearing 100 per cent of the weight. Knee bent in a one-quarter squat.

3. Right foot—points northwest, toe kicking imaginary opponent's knee. Sole of foot and thigh parallel to ground. Angle behind knee about 120 degrees.

4. Hips and shoulders—face west.

5. Right hand—edge extended toward northwest, fingers pointing up at about eye level. Arm in line with right leg. Elbow bent about 120 degrees.

6. Left hand—extended to the left and slightly forward of left shoulder, palm facing out (west) and fingers pointing up at about eye level. Elbow bent about 120 degrees.

34. Separate Left Foot

A. Withdraw your right foot to your right knee and then step diagonally forward toward the right (northwest), setting the heel down first (Figure 120). Shift all of your weight to your right foot. As the weight shifts, lower your hands and point them diagonally toward the left (southwest). At the same time, turn your head toward the southwest and raise the heel of your left foot, leaving just the toe touching. When 100 per cent of your weight is on your right foot, the left hand points southwest, slightly below shoulder height, palm down, with elbow bent to form an angle somewhat greater than 90 degrees. The right hand is palm up just below and to the right of the left elbow (Figure 121).

B. Rotate your body to the right (clockwise) until you face northwest. Simultaneously, lower your hands and then raise them in a circle beyond your right side and shoulder (Figure 122).

C. Turn your body to the left (counterclockwise). At the same time, bring your hands forward to form an X in front of and about eight inches from your chest, slightly below shoulder height, right hand closer to your chest and above the left wrist. As your hands meet in front of your chest, move your left foot forward and set it down without weight, only the toe touching, pointing diagonally left (southwest). Time your movements so that the hands and the left foot reach their terminal positions at the same moment (Figure 123).

D. Just as your body completes its counterclockwise rotation and faces west, raise your left foot in a kick to the southwest, aimed at an opponent's knee. Simultaneously, rotate your hands to turn the palms outward, and separate the hands, extending the left hand toward the southwest and the right toward your right side. Both hands have their fingers pointing up. The left hand is in line with the left leg and the right hand is to the right and slightly forward of your right shoulder (Figure 124).

Position Check

1. Head and eyes—face southwest in direction of kick.

2. Right foot—points northwest, bearing 100 per cent of the weight. Knee bent in a one-quarter squat.

3. Left foot—points southwest, toe kicking opponent's knee. Sole of foot and thigh parallel to ground. Angle behind knee about 120 degrees.

4. Hips and shoulders—face west.

5. Left hand—edge extends toward southwest, fingers pointing up at about eye level. Arm in line with left leg. Elbow bent about 120 degrees.

6. Right hand—extends to the right and slightly forward of right shoulder, palm facing out (west) and fingers pointing up at about eye level. Elbow bent about 120 degrees.

35. Turn and Kick with Heel

125

126

A. Bring your left foot to your right knee. At the same time, rotate your body to the right (clockwise) until you face northwest, and lower your hands toward your right side (Figure 125).

B. Rotate your body to the left (counterclockwise) by pivoting on your right heel until your right foot points south. As your body turns, bring your hands up in an X in front of your chest, slightly below shoulder level. The right hand is to the outside of the left, with palms facing your body (Figure 126).

C. Continue rotating your body until you face southeast. Simultaneously, bring your left knee farther to the left until it points east, and deliver a kick with your heel to an imaginary opponent's midsection. As your foot kicks out, separate your hands, extending the left hand toward the east in line with your left leg, and the right hand to a point to the right and slightly forward of your right shoulder (Figure 127).

127

Position Check

1. Head and eyes—face east.

2. Right foot—points south, bearing 100 per cent of the weight. Knee bent in a one-quarter squat.

3. Left foot—points east, toes pulled up toward the shin and heel kicking opponent's midsection. Keep knee relaxed and avoid straightening it completely as you kick.

4. Hips and shoulders—face southeast.

5. Left hand—edge extends east and forearm is in line with left leg. Fingers point up at about eye level. Elbow bent about 120 degrees.

6. Right hand—extends to right and slightly forward of right shoulder, fingers pointing up at about eye level. Palm turned out, facing south. Elbow bent about 90 degrees.

36. Brush Knee and Twist Step (Left)

A. Withdraw your left foot to your right knee and your left hand to a point near your right hip, palm facing your body. At the same time, allow your right hand to drop forward at the wrist until the palm faces down and fingers point east at about ear level (Figure 128).

B. Step forward and to the left with your left foot and set it down, heel first, pointing east (Figure 129). Transfer 70 per cent of your weight to your left foot and revolve your body to the left (counterclockwise) until you face directly east. At the same time, bring your right hand forward to a point in front of your right shoulder and move your left hand, fingers down and palm facing your body, across your groin area, stopping just to the left

128

of your left thigh. As your body and hands end their movement, turn your right toe inward 45 degrees (Figure 130).

Position Check

1. Feet, legs, body, and head fulfill requirements of 70-30 position. (See p. 33.) Direction is east.

2. Right hand—in front of right shoulder, palm facing out (east), wrist and top of shoulder along same horizontal plane. Elbow bent 90 degrees.

3. Left hand—just to left of left thigh. Palm faces down and to rear. Elbow slightly bent.

129

130

37. Brush Knee and Twist Step (Right)

A.   Shift your weight to your right foot, and turn your body and your left toe 45 degrees to the left (northeast). At the same time, revolve your left hand until the palm is up and move your right hand, palm down, toward your left side at slightly below shoulder level until it is directly over the left hand (Figure 131).

B.   Transfer your weight to your left foot. Simultaneously, lower your right hand toward your right thigh, palm facing the body and fingers pointing down. As the right drops, circle your left hand back and up to a point level with your ear and turn it over, palm down, with the fingers pointing ahead (east). After all of your weight is on your left foot and just before your hands reach their positions, step straight forward with your right foot and place the heel on the ground, without weight, foot pointing east. Time your movements so that both hands and the heel of your right foot reach their terminal positions at the same instant (Figure 132).

133

C. Transfer 70 per cent of your weight to your right foot and rotate your body to the right (clockwise) until you face directly east. At the same time, bring your left hand forward to a point in front of your left shoulder and move your right hand, fingers down and palm facing your body, across your groin area, stopping just to the right of your right thigh (Figure 133).

Position Check

1. Feet, legs, body, and head fulfill requirements of 70-30 position. (See p. 33.) Direction is east.

2. Left hand—in front of left shoulder, palm facing out (east), wrist and top of shoulder along same horizontal plane. Elbow bent 90 degrees.

3. Right hand—just to right of right thigh. Palm faces down and to rear. Elbow slightly bent.

38. Step Forward and Punch

A. Shift your weight to your left foot and turn your body and your right toe 45 degrees to the right (southeast). At the same time, lower your left hand, palm facing the body and fingers pointing down, to a point near the front of your right thigh (Figure 134).

B. Transfer your weight to your right foot. Simultaneously, raise your right hand to a point above and slightly behind your right hip, ending there in a loosely held fist with knuckles down. Just before your right fist reaches this position, step straight forward with your left foot and place the heel on the ground, without weight, foot pointing east. Time your movements so that your right hand and the heel of your left foot reach their terminal positions at the same instant (Figure 135).

C. Shift 70 per cent of your weight to your left foot, lower your body slightly, and rotate it to the left (counterclockwise) until you face directly

134

east. At the same time, punch diagonally downward with your right hand. Simultaneously, move your left hand, fingers down and palm facing the body, across your pelvic area, stopping just to the left of your left thigh (Figure 136).

Position Check

1. Feet, legs, body, and head fulfill requirements of 70-30 position. (See p. 33.) Direction is east. There is a slight variation, however, caused by the direction of the punch. Thus, the eyes look in the direction of the punch and the head and upper body are inclined slightly forward. In addition, the knees are bent a bit more than the usual one-quarter squat.

2. Right hand—in a loosely held vertical fist, in center of body. Wrist about six inches lower than elbow. Elbow bent 120 degrees.

3. Left hand—just to the left of left thigh. Palm faces down and to rear. Elbow slightly bent.

135

136

39. *Grasp Bird's Tail (Ward Off with Right Hand)*

137

138

A. Shift your weight to your right foot and turn your body and your left toe 45 degrees to the left (northeast). As your weight shifts, raise your body slightly until your right knee is again in a one-quarter squat. At the same time, open your right hand and withdraw it toward your left thigh, fingers pointing down and palm facing your body (Figure 137).

B. Transfer your weight to your left foot. Begin to raise your hands toward the center of your body at shoulder level, right palm facing you and left facing down. When your hands are about halfway to your shoulders, step straight forward with your right foot and place the heel on the ground, without weight, foot pointing east (Figure 138).

139

C. Shift 70 per cent of your weight to your right foot and rotate your body to the right (clockwise) until you face directly east. At the same time, complete the hand movements necessary to this position. (See Position 4; Figure 139.)

Position Check

Refer to Position Check for Position 4.

40. *Grasp Bird's Tail (Rollback and Press)*

This movement repeats Position 5 (Figures 140, 141, 142, 143).

142

143

41. Grasp Bird's Tail (Push)

This movement repeats Position 6 (Figures 144, 145).

144

145

42. Single Whip

This movement repeats Position 7 (Figures 146, 147, 148, 149, 150, 151, 152).

43. Fair Lady Works at Shuttles (Right)

A. Shift your weight to your right foot, rotate your body to the right (clockwise), turn your left foot to the right until it points north, and lower your left hand toward your lower abdomen, fingers pointing down. Do all of these movements simultaneously (Figure 153).

B. Transfer your weight to your left foot and continue to rotate your body to the right (clockwise) until it faces northeast. At the same time, release the "hook" formed by your right hand and bring the hand toward your face, palm turned toward you and fingers pointing up. As the right hand moves toward you, the left continues upward to end, palm up, near your right elbow. When enough weight has left your right foot, as a result of your shift to the left, pivot on the right toe until the foot points in the direction you face (northeast) (Figure 154).

C. Move your right foot to the right and set it down, in line with the back of your left foot, heel first, pointing slightly south of east (Figure 155). Shift your weight to the right foot and rotate your body somewhat more to the right (clockwise) until you face east. Take a step with your left foot to the northeast and set the foot down, heel first and pointing northeast. As your foot moves out, extend your left hand toward the northeast (Figure 156).

D. Transfer 70 per cent of your weight to your left foot. As weight shifts, rotate your body to the left (counterclockwise) until you face northeast. Use this rotation to withdraw your left hand to a point in front of your forehead, palm facing out, and to move your right hand forward until it is in front of your face and below the left hand, palm turned out. In addition, when enough weight has shifted to your left foot, turn your right toe slightly inward until it points east. Insure that all movement ends at the same instant (Figure 157).

Position Check

1. Feet, legs, body, and head fulfill requirements of 70-30 position. (See p. 33.) Direction is northeast.

2. Left hand—in front of and slightly above forehead, fingers pointing diagonally upward, palm facing out. Elbow bent 90 degrees.

3. Right hand—in front of face, a few inches farther out than left hand. Palm turned out and fingers pointing up. Elbow bent 90 degrees.

44. *Fair Lady Works at Shuttles (Left)*

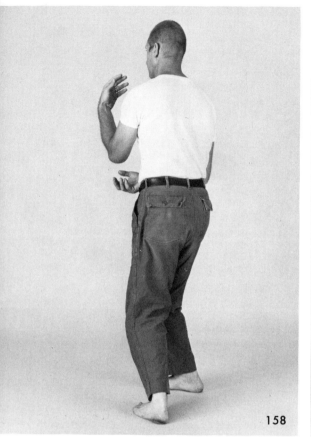
158

159

A.   Shift your weight to your right foot, rotate your body to the right (clockwise), and turn your left toe to the right until it points south. Simultaneously, lower your hands and rotate them until the left palm faces you with fingers pointing up, the tips at about chin level. The right hand is palm up near your left elbow (Figure 158).

B.   Transfer your weight to your left foot, continue to rotate your body to the right (clockwise), and pivot on the right toe so the right foot points in the direction you face (Figure 159). When your body has rotated as far to the right as possible, take a long step with the right foot to your right rear, setting the heel down, without weight, foot pointing northwest (Figure 160).

C.   Shift 70 per cent of your weight to your right foot. As weight shifts, extend your right hand, fingers leading, toward the northwest. At the same time, continue rotating your body clockwise until it faces northwest. Use this

rotation to move your left hand forward in front of your face, palm turned out, and to withdraw your right hand to a point in front of your forehead, palm outward. In addition, turn your left toe inward 90 degrees until it points west. Insure that all movement ends at the same instant (Figure 161).

Position Check

1. Feet, legs, body, and head fulfill requirements of 70-30 position. (See p. 33.) Direction is northwest.

2. Right hand in front of and slightly above forehead, fingers pointing diagonally upward, palm facing out. Elbow bent 90 degrees.

3. Left hand—in front of face, a few inches farther out than right hand. Palm turned out and fingers pointing up. Elbow bent 90 degrees.

45. Fair Lady Works at Shuttles (Right)

This position is essentially a repetition of Position 43 in a different direction.

A.   Transfer your weight to your left foot. As your weight shifts, lower your hands and rotate them until the right palm faces you with fingers pointing up, the tips at about chin level. The left hand is palm up near your right elbow (Figure 162).

B.   Take a diagonal step toward the west with your right foot and set it down, heel first, pointing northwest and directly in front (west) of your left foot (Figure 163). Shift your weight to your right foot.

C.   Step diagonally toward the left (southwest) with your left foot and set the heel down first, foot pointing southwest. As your foot moves forward, extend your left hand toward the southwest (Figure 164). Transfer

162

163

70 per cent of your weight to your left foot. Simultaneously, rotate your body to the left (counterclockwise) until you face southwest. Use this rotation to withdraw your left hand to a point in front of your forehead, palm facing out, and to extend your right hand until it is in front of your face and below the left, palm turned out. As the movement concludes, turn your right toe inward 45 degrees (Figure 165).

Position Check

1. Feet, legs, body, and head fulfill requirements of 70-30 position. (See p. 33.) Direction is southwest.

2. Left hand—in front of and slightly above forehead, fingers pointing diagonally upward, palm facing out. Elbow bent 90 degrees.

3. Right hand—in front of face, a few inches farther out than the left hand. Palm turned out and fingers pointing up. Elbow bent 90 degrees.

164

165

46. Fair Lady Works at Shuttles (Left)

This position repeats Position 44 in a different direction.

A. Shift your weight to your right foot, rotate your body to the right (clockwise) and turn your left toe to the right until it points north. Simultaneously, lower your hands and rotate them until the left palm faces you with fingers pointing up, the tips at about chin level. The right hand is palm up near your left elbow (Figure 166).

B. Transfer your weight to your left foot, continue to rotate your body to the right (clockwise), and pivot on the right toe so the right foot points in the direction you face (Figure 167). When your body has rotated as far to the right as possible, take a long step with the right foot to your right rear, setting the heel down, without weight, foot pointing southeast (Figure 168).

166

167

C.   Shift 70 per cent of your weight to your right foot. As weight shifts, extend your right hand, fingers leading, toward the southeast. At the same time, continue rotating your body clockwise until you face southeast. Use this rotation to move your left hand forward in front of your face, palm turned out, and to withdraw your right hand to a point in front of your forehead, palm outward. As movement ends, turn your left toe inward 90 degrees until it points east (Figure 169).

Position Check

1.   Feet, legs, body, and head fulfill requirements of 70-30 position. (See p. 33.) Direction is southeast.

2.   Right hand—in front of and slightly above forehead, fingers pointing diagonally upward, palm facing out. Elbow bent 90 degrees.

3.   Left hand—in front of face, a few inches farther out than right hand. Palm turned out and fingers pointing up. Elbow bent 90 degrees.

168

169

47. Grasp Bird's Tail (Ward Off with Left Hand)

170

171

Shift all of your weight to your right foot, allowing your left heel to leave the ground. Simultaneously, lower your hands, revolving them, until your right hand is palm down at armpit level in the center of your body and your left hand is palm up in front of your lower abdomen, directly below the right. The hands appear to be holding a ball of air between them (Figure 170). Just before your weight is completely on your right foot, rotate

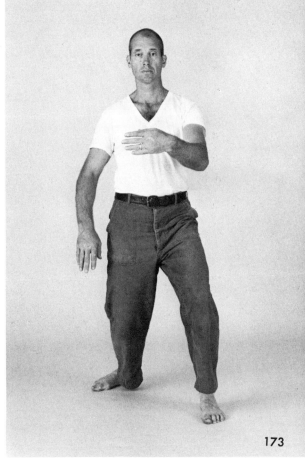

172

173

your body to the left (counterclockwise), then pick up your left foot, move it a few inches to the left (west), and set it down, heel first, pointing north (Figure 171).

Follow the directions given earlier for Position 3, beginning with 3D. Note that at the conclusion, the right toe must turn inward 90 degrees instead of 45 (Figures 172, 173).

48. Grasp Bird's Tail (Ward Off with Right Hand)

174

175

This movement repeats Position 4 (Figures 174, 175, 176, 177).

176

177

49. Grasp Bird's Tail (Rollback and Press)

This movement repeats Position 5 (Figures 178, 179, 180, 181).

180

181

50. *Grasp Bird's Tail (Push)*

182

This movement repeats Position 6 (Figures 182, 183).

51. Single Whip

This movement repeats Position 7 (Figures 184, 185, 186, 187, 188, 189, 190).

186

187

189

190

52. Snake Creeps Down

191

This movement repeats Position 30 (Figures 191, 192, 193).

192

193

53. *Step Forward to Form Seven Stars*

194

195

A. Shift your weight to your left foot and begin to rise. Simultaneously, raise your left hand, fingers leading, to a point slightly above and forward of your left shoulder (Figure 194). Rotate your body to the left (counterclockwise) until you face west, and turn your right toe inward 45 degrees until it points northwest (Figure 195).

B. When 100 per cent of your weight reaches your left foot, draw your right foot forward and, releasing its "hook," bring your right hand in toward the front of your right hip (Figure 196). Continue to step forward with the right foot and set it down forward of your left, without any weight, only the toe touching the ground. At the same time, move your right hand forward and up, form a loose fist with both hands and cross the hands at the wrist in front of you at slightly below chin level (Figure 197).

Position Check

1. Head and eyes—face west.

2. Left foot—points southwest, bearing 100 per cent of the weight. Knee bent in a one-quarter squat.

3. Right foot—points west, bearing no weight, only the toe touching the ground. Knee slightly bent. If the foot were drawn straight back, it would just avoid hitting the heel of the left foot.

4. Hips and shoulders—face west.

5. Hands—crossed at the wrists in the center of your body at slightly below chin level. Hands have formed loosely held fists. Left fist about eight inches from chin and closer to you than right. Bottom of fist facing out.

54. Retreat to Ride Tiger

198

199

A. Step to your right rear with your right foot, place the foot on the ground, toe first, pointing diagonally right (northwest) (Figure 198), and shift your weight to it. As weight shifts, open your hands and lower them, palms touching, with the right palm facing up and the left down (Figure 199).

B. When your hands reach your lower abdomen, rotate your body to the right (clockwise) until it faces northwest. Simultaneously, circle your right hand upward to the right rear and move your left downward in the direction of your left thigh (Figure 200). Rotate your body to the left (counterclockwise) until you face west. Use this rotation to bring your right hand, fingers up and palm facing forward, to a point to the right of your right ear. Also, move your left hand, fingers pointing down, just to the left of your left thigh. Just before you complete this movement, shift your left foot to the right and set it down in front of you without weight, only the toe touching (Figure 201).

200   201

Position Check

1. Head and eyes—face west.

2. Right foot—points northwest, bearing 100 per cent of the weight. Knee bent in a one-quarter squat.

3. Left foot—points west, bearing no weight, only the toe touching the ground. Knee slightly bent. If the foot were drawn straight back, it would just avoid hitting the right heel.

4. Hips and shoulders—face west.

5. Right hand—across from right ear, palm facing forward (west), fingers pointing up. Forearm almost vertical.

6. Left hand—just to left of left thigh, fingers pointing down, palm facing downward to rear. Elbow slightly bent.

55. *Turn Around and Kick Horizontally*

A. Turn your body slightly to the left (counterclockwise). As you turn, bring your left hand to your left rear with the palm facing forward (west) and fingers pointing down, and move your right hand, palm in, near your left hip (Figure 202).

B. Pivot on the ball of your right foot and rotate your body to the right (clockwise) in a full circle (360 degrees), using your left arm and left side to generate momentum. As you rotate, sweep your left foot a fraction of an inch above the ground. When your body has turned somewhat more than halfway (210 degrees), set your left heel down (Figure 203) and, as you continue turning, begin to shift your weight to the left foot. Continue your turn until you again face west. At this point, all your weight is on your left foot and the foot points southwest. Your right toe just touches the ground in front of, and slightly to the right of, your left foot. Hands are at solar plexus level in front of you, shoulder width apart, palms down (Figure 204).

C. Raise your right foot and, with a slight hip rotation, sweep the toe across your palms from left to right (clockwise). Insure that your right knee is raised high enough to avoid bending forward or dropping your hands to contact your toe (Figure 205).

Position Check

1. Head and eyes—face west.

2. Left foot—points southwest, bearing 100 per cent of the weight. Knee bent in a one-quarter squat.

3. Right foot—in front of you, toe up, sweeping from left to right (clockwise) across your palms.

4. Hips and shoulders—face west.

5. Hands—at solar plexus level, palms down, shoulder width apart, with fingers pointing straight ahead (west).

204

205

56. Bend Bow and Shoot Tiger

A. As your right foot completes its circle, bring it to your left knee (Figure 206) and then step forward with it diagonally to the right (northwest). Set the heel down first, foot pointing northwest, and begin to shift weight to the foot (Figure 207). As weight shifts, rotate your body to the right (clockwise) as far as possible, and first lower and then raise your hands in a circle to your right side (Figure 208). Form the hands into loose fists as they rise (Figure 209).

B. Reverse the rotation of your body (counterclockwise) until you face northwest. This results in only a slight turn. Use this turn to bring your fists forward, both pointing toward the southwest, the right six inches forward of the face at nose level and the left 12 inches forward of the left hip. As your hands move forward, look in the direction of the punches and turn your left toe inward 45 degrees until the foot points west (Figure 210).

Position Check

1. Head and eyes—face southwest.

2. Feet, legs, and body fulfill requirements of the 70-30 position. (See p. 32.) Direction is northwest.

3. Right hand—held vertically in a loose fist at nose level, six inches forward of face, forearm parallel to ground, and elbow bent 90 degrees. Forearm and fist point southwest.

4. Left hand—held vertically in a loose fist at hip level, twelve inches in front of left hip, forearm parallel to ground, and elbow bent somewhat more than 90 degrees. Forearm and fist point southwest.

143

57. Deflect Downward, Parry, and Punch

Holding your position, but turning your head to the right to look northwest, shift all of your weight to your right foot, lift the left foot slightly off the ground (Figure 211), turn it 45 degrees to the left, and set it down pointing southwest. Shift your weight to your left foot. As weight shifts, lower and revolve your right forearm and open your left hand, turning it until the palm is up near your right elbow at abdominal level (Figure 212). Rotate your body to the left (counterclockwise), turn your right toe inward toward the left, and lower your hands toward your left thigh, the left hand open and the right remaining loosely clenched (Figure 213). Move your right foot a few inches to the left and set it down, heel first, pointing diagonally right (northwest) (Figure 214). Transfer your weight to your right foot, allowing your hands to lag behind you and circle upward (Figure 215).

Continue by following the instructions for Position 14, beginning with 14D (Figures 216, 217).

214

215

216

217

58.　*Apparent Closure*

218

219

This movement repeats Position 15 (Figures 218, 219, 220, 221).

220

221

59. *Cross Hands*

222

This movement repeats Position 16 (Figures 222, 223, 224).

223

224

60. Conclusion

225

When your weight is evenly distributed between your two feet, straighten, but do not lock, your knees, and lower your hands to your sides, palms facing the rear. Co-ordinate your rise with the lowering of your hands so that all movement ends at the same instant. Your position is again that at the end of Position 1 (Figure 225).

TAI CHI
FOR SELF-DEFENSE
PUSH-HANDS

As explained elsewhere in this book, doing the tai chi form lays some of the groundwork—balance, body flexibility, relaxation, and timing—that is necessary for coping successfully with an assailant. In addition, we gradually acquire the leg strength essential to any kind of physical activity which involves the whole body. However, a knowledge of the form alone will not enable us to defend ourselves from physical attack. If our intention is to learn self-defense, we must practice attacking and defending with a partner.

Over the centuries, the martial artists responsible for the development of tai chi constructed a method of dealing with an assailant that relies for success on sensitivity and flexibility instead of on strength. Whether defending or attacking, the emphasis is on restraint in the use of strength. The reason for this approach is that in many cases we cannot be absolutely certain that we have our opponent in a disadvantageous position. If we think that he is at our mercy and commit ourselves totally to an attack, we may find that we have misread the situation and that our overcommitment causes us to lose balance and suffer defeat.

These early masters devised a system of defense and attack that avoids overcommitment in any sense. In addition, this method relies on a stance which has some of the characteristics of bamboo or of some other tree that is firmly rooted and balanced but has flexibility and resilience in its trunk (hips and torso) and branches (arms). Thus, when someone attempts some form of attack against us, we must prevent him from applying his strength to any part of our body. One way to avoid an attack is to shift the body in such a way that the assailant is never presented with a solid surface upon which to exert strength. However, if we are to offer the opponent no attacking point, we must know or sense the direction and force of his attack. This calls for the development of extreme sensitivity at any point of the body that touches the opponent. If we realize that in a realistic situation the duration of such contact is only a split second, we can begin to understand the difficulty of acquiring such refined technique.

Fortunately, a method of practice was devised which allows us gradually to develop the kind of ability in question. It is called "push-hands." In push-hands we face a partner from a fixed stance and, using only the minimum of strength, attempt to push him off balance. The training partner's intention is to retain his balance, without moving his feet, and to do whatever he can, short of relying on strength, to disturb ours. As with the form, movements are performed slowly because learning proceeds most rapidly when we have sufficient time in which to determine the appropriate defense and counterattack.

Nevertheless, training in push-hands alone will not enable us to adequately defend ourselves against an assailant who is strong and agile or is himself skilled in some martial art. This is because the technique we develop in push-hands is acquired under controlled conditions. We must refrain from moving our feet and we must practice slowly. In a real situation, an attack might take the form of combinations of rapid blows and kicks followed by a throw. Therefore, it is necessary after some time to become familiar with the quick and mobile attacks used in actual fighting. However, in dealing with stronger and faster attacks, we must continue to observe tai chi principles and insure that our movements are free of unnecessary tension and strength. On the other hand, this advanced training does not preclude moving the feet in any direction to assume a more favorable position from which to attack or defend.

Although this kind of self-defense training is recommended, we should realize that ultimately we make contact with an opponent from the fixed position we assume in push-hands. It is clear also that too great an emphasis on moving the feet, to avoid an attack, reduces reliance on and, consequently, inhibits development of body flexibility. Thus, the greater part of our self-defense practice in tai chi should be of the fixed position push-hands kind, but it should not exclude familiarity with stronger and faster attacks.

Observe the following principles and considerations for optimum progress in push-hands.

1. *Avoid using strength.*

Do not force the opponent in any direction or resist his attack by directly opposing it. In such a situation the stronger man would push the weaker off balance, but neither would be refining his technique. If you are defending and your opponent, thinking he has found a solid point to attack, attempts to push or strike you, move your body in such a way that when the attack comes the imagined surface is no longer there or is not solid. The result is usually some loss of balance by the attacker. This weakness can be used to counterattack. Under these conditions, only a minimum amount of strength need be used to counter because the opponent's position has become weak and unstable.

If the attacker wishes to avoid the foregoing adverse situation, he must be tentative in his attack. He must insure that in his attempt to push or strike some point of his opponent's body he does .not overextend and lose his balance. He must avoid tightening or stiffening his arms and shoulders at any time to prevent the arms being used by the opponent as handles to move his body and disturb his balance. If arms are kept relaxed and flexible, it is difficult for the defender to grasp them and use them to control the attacker. Moreover, relaxed arms can more easily transmit the force generated by the legs and body to the target. Finally, the attacker must be fairly certain of the opponent's vulnerability before he commits himself to an attack.

2. *Maintain a low center of gravity.*

Keep your knees bent as your weight shifts from one foot to the other. In general, if your center of gravity is lower than your opponent's, he encounters difficulty in upsetting your balance. It is also easier to break the opponent's balance if you attack from a position lower than his. However, too much bend in the knees results in a static position which sacrifices flexibility of movement. As you practice, become aware of the degree of knee bend that appears most advantageous, or seems optimum.

Relaxing the body to the fullest possible extent also adds to stability. Although the body is not appreciably lowered by relaxing it, the effect of this action is similar to a drop in the center of gravity. Another contribution to the stability and solidity of your stance is to imagine your feet have roots which extend downward into the ground. This way of thinking comes more easily if the body is relaxed and the body weight is permitted to go directly into the feet and into the ground.

3. *Keep the center of gravity inside the base area formed by the feet.*

If the feet are thought of as the diagonally opposite corners of a rectangle, prevent your center of gravity from falling outside this base area. It is obvious that failure to observe this rule will result in loss of stability and balance. Of course, the feet may shift to increase the dimensions of the rectangle if you sense loss of balance, but in push-hands you are attempting to develop an awareness of possible instability early enough to take action that will make a foot movement unnecessary.

4. *Keep your body perpendicular to the ground.*

This principle is related to the preceding one in that leaning in any direction will move the center of gravity in that direction. If you lean too far in a particular direction, the center of gravity will fall outside your base area and you will lose your balance. In addition, leaning in a certain direction reduces the option for movement in other directions. On the other hand, if your body remains perpendicular to the ground, you can more easily make the small adjustments in any direction that you sense necessary to avoid presenting the opponent with a solid surface for his attack.

5. *Avoid distributing body weight equally between the feet.*

"Double-weighting" is the term used to refer to a condition where each foot carries an equal amount of weight. Under these circumstances some degree of agility is lost, providing the opponent an opportunity for a successful attack. The prescribed form for push-hands requires a constant shift of weight from one foot to the other as training partners alternately attack and defend. If an attack is timed to coincide with the moment in the opponent's movement when his weight is equal between the feet, the attack has a good chance of success.

Double-weighting can also refer to pushing or attacking with an equal amount of force in each hand. An attack of this nature is relatively weak. When the opponent shifts his body to avoid the attack it is very difficult for both hands to remain on target. Usually in this situation, when one hand loses the target, the other also is misdirected, usually resulting in an over-extension and a loss of balance.

6. *When the greater part of your weight is on one foot or the greater proportion of thrust is exerted by one foot, attack with the hand on the opposite side of the body.*

As an example, if the right foot carries more weight or delivers more thrust than the left, attack with the left hand. This principle is related to the foregoing, which states that an attack which delivers force equally by both hands at the same time is ineffective. If the present principle is observed, it is impossible to attack with equal force in both hands. Further, to attack with the left hand when the greater part of your weight is on, or thrust comes from, your left foot is ineffective because you are unable to fully transmit the body's force to the target. The usual result of this action is loss of stability.

154

Pushing hands with the above principle in mind helps develop a better understanding of the concept of the "full" and "empty" leg and arm in the form. Thus, when the right leg is "full," or supports most of the weight, the left arm is also "full."

7. *Avoid placing all of your weight on one foot.*

Just as placing your weight equally between the two feet reduces agility, placing all of the weight on only one foot also weakens your position. This weakness occurs because the base area formed by the feet becomes severely reduced when all of the weight moves to one foot. If the opponent sticks to you and follows your body as it shifts to one foot, you will be cornered and have almost no chance to escape. In such a situation the defender often attempts to resist the opponent's attack because he has exhausted other possibilities. Opponents are then presented a solid surface to attack. Therefore, in push-hands the ideal stance for both defense and attack is to have more weight on one foot than on the other, but not to the extent of completely emptying one foot of weight.

8. *Use the mind as well as the body in your training.*

In general, the mind should not become preoccupied with any one aspect of attack or defense, but should have the ability to immediately register and respond to any change in the opponent's actions. However, when an attacking opportunity comes, focus all of your mind force on the point to be attacked. This change takes place in an instant, after which the mind immediately resumes its attitude of alert receptivity.

9. *Develop a sense of timing.*

It seems clear that any attack or defense will fail if it does not come at the very moment of a weakness in the opponent's position. Choose the right moment to respond to some defect in the opponent's attack or defense and you will defeat him.

Timing must also be considered from the standpoint of your body's ability to generate and transmit force. Any movement achieves maximum effect if your foot and leg thrust strongly into the ground, and no blockage caused by tension occurs in any part of the body. The existence of such a block reduces the amount of force that will reach the target. Ideally, this force acts in a wavelike manner, flowing upward from the foot and leg, being directed by the hips, passing through the shoulder, and moving down the arm to the hand to finally explode on the target. This movement takes place in a split second. Correct timing insures the unbroken wavelike effect of this force, with consequent maximum impact on the target.

10.   *Consider every push a potentially incapacitating attack.*

If you push your opponent in accordance with the foregoing considerations, you will over the years begin to sense the development in you of a capacity to deliver a devastating attack. This ability must be carefully nurtured by attempting to make your slow-motion pushes as perfect as possible. Do not think it enough to merely have your opponent lose a degree of stability when you push, but try to attack him so that both of his feet leave the ground. If your push is correctly delivered, you will be able to generate the kind of explosive power that, fully unleashed, could cause severe injury to the internal organs of the opponent.

For best results in defense, you must think of the opponent as possessing this same potential for doing damage. Therefore, he must not be permitted a surface which will receive his attack. If possible, move your body in such a way that the opponent is unable to place his hands on it.

Push-Hands (Single-Hand)

226

Using only one hand to attack and defend provides a good introduction to pushing with two hands. The various principles involved in pushing hands are more easily recognized and appreciated by students if they need not immediately embark on learning the more complicated hand movements of the two-hand push-hands. Above all, sticking or lightly adhering to the opponent's hand, no matter where it moves, is most easily learned if only one hand is used to push. Also important is the growth of hip and body flexibility gained in the course of evading the opponent's one-hand attack.

To do push-hands with one hand, opponents stand facing one another in the "70-30" stance. For convenience, let us call the man on the viewer's right (man without beard) "A" and his opponent "B." A's front (right) foot is positioned so that his toe is even with B's heel and his heel even with B's toe. In addition, A's front (right) foot is in line with B's back (left) foot and his back foot even with B's front (Figure 226).

157

A raises his right hand in front of his solar plexus at a distance of about eight inches from the body (Figure 227).

227

B places the back of his right hand lightly against the back of A's right hand (Figure 228).

228

The opponent's hands must stay together throughout any movement as if they were magnetically attracted to one another. An increase of hand pressure by one is instantly countered by a decrease on the part of the other so that hand pressure remains constant. Their left hands hang at their sides and are not brought into play. A attacks by shifting his weight a bit more forward and increasing the pressure on B's hand, directing an attack at B's solar plexus (Figure 229).

229

B shifts his weight to the rear and rotates his body clockwise, allowing A's hand to miss the target and go harmlessly by (Figure 230).

230

A realizes his mistake and
begins to withdraw his hand
(Figure 231).

231

B follows this withdrawal by
adhering to A's hand and
becomes the attacker. To attack,
B shifts his weight forward and
increases the pressure on A's
hand, aiming for A's solar plexus
(Figure 232).

232

A shifts his weight to the rear and rotates his body clockwise, causing B's hand to miss its target (Figure 233).

233

B withdraws and A again becomes the attacker (Figure 234).

This alternation of attack and defense can be continued indefinitely. If the left foot is forward instead of the right, use the left hand to push. The hands describe an ellipse. If the right foot is forward, move the right hand traveling along the path of this ellipse in a counterclockwise direction. If the left foot is advanced, the left hand travels clockwise. Rotate your body to the maximum possible extent in the required direction as you defend. In addition, as you shift most of your weight to the back foot, maintain a low center of gravity by bending that knee until it is at least in a one-quarter squat.

234

Push-Hands (Two-Hands)

For convenience, let us call the person on the viewer's right (man without beard) "A" and his opponent "B." Opponents stand facing one another squarely in the "70-30" stance. A's front (right) foot is positioned so that his toe is even with B's heel and his heel even with B's toe. In addition, A's front (right) foot is in line with B's back (left) foot and his back foot is in line with B's front (Figure 235).

235

A places his left forearm in front of his body at solar plexus level at a distance of about eight inches from the body. Palm of the left hand faces the body (Figure 236).

236

B places his left palm on A's left wrist and his right palm on A's left elbow (Figure 237).

As B makes contact with A's forearm, A places his right elbow lightly against B's left elbow or forearm. A's forearm is almost vertical and fingers point up (Figure 238).

B begins to push A to the rear. A shifts his weight toward his back foot and rotates his body counterclockwise. Simultaneously, A's right elbow returns just as much force to B's left arm as B is using in his attack (Figure 239).

239

240

Were B to continue with his push in the direction he began, he would lose his balance (Figure 240).

The push-hands form prescribes that B become aware that he is no longer focusing on the center of A's body and that he is beginning to lose his balance. B therefore changes the direction of his attack. Thus, B rotates the hand on A's wrist until the back of the hand, instead of the palm, touches A's wrist (Figure 241).

241

Next, B places his right palm against the heel of his left palm and attacks the new location of A's center (Figure 242).

242

A responds to B's change of direction by rotating his body clockwise, shifting his weight a bit more to his back foot and dropping his right hand to the back of B's right wrist (Figure 243).

243

Again, were B to continue his attack, he would lose his balance (Figure 244).

244

B realizes his predicament and withdraws, assuming the role of the defender. B's right forearm revolves and moves so that it is about eight inches in front of his body at solar plexus height, palm facing the body (Figure 245).

245

As B withdraws, A maintains contact with him and becomes the attacker by revolving his right hand on B's right wrist and placing his left palm on B's right elbow. As A begins to push B to the rear, B's left elbow lightly touches A's right forearm near the elbow. B's left forearm is almost vertical and his fingers point up (Figure 246).

246

B shifts his weight to his back foot and rotates his body clockwise. Simultaneously, B's left elbow returns just as much force to A's right arm as A is using in his attack (Figure 247).

247

Were A to continue attacking without changing direction, he would lose his balance (Figure 248).

248

A knows he must change the
direction of his attack.
Consequently, he rotates the hand
on B's wrist until the back of the
hand, instead of the palm, touches
B's wrist (Figure 249).

249

Next, A places his left hand on
the heel of his right palm and
attacks the new location of B's
center (Figure 250).

250

B responds to A's change of direction by rotating his body counterclockwise, shifting his weight more to his back foot, and dropping his left hand to the back of A's left wrist (Figure 251).

251

Again, were A to continue his attack, he would lose his balance (Figure 252).

252

A must withdraw and B becomes the attacker (Figure 253).

This basic pattern can be repeated endlessly. Instead of beginning with the left forearm extended horizontally in front of the body, A might have placed the right forearm there. Also, A's left instead of his right foot could be advanced. During practice, avoid favoring one side of your body over the other. Develop the ability to use your left and right side with equal facility.

253

ATTITUDES
THAT FURTHER DEVELOPMENT

Tai chi, whether done primarily as an exercise, as meditation, or as self-defense, must be practiced almost daily over the years if we are to realize the many benefits such training can give us. Ideally, all three aspects of this art—exercise, meditation, and self-defense—are not thought of as separate but are usually given equal emphasis by those who practice diligently.

If we are to achieve optimum development in tai chi, we must find a qualified teacher. This search is sometimes difficult. Convenience of location should not be an important criterion. A teacher's reputation is often a useful basis of selection. Also, we might choose a teacher on the recommendation of a friend whose opinion we respect and who has studied with him. Whatever the method of choice, it is usually best to observe a class before coming to a decision. Our first impression of a teacher's capabilities should give us a fairly good idea whether or not he has something to teach. We will also know whether or not we can learn from him. Once we have placed ourselves in the hands of a teacher we must trust him to direct us toward the correct path.

If the practice of a particular art is considered to lead to some sort of inner development or self-realization, a teacher of that art can be expected to demonstrate, in his general manner and outlook, the fruits of long training. However, it does not further the student's or the teacher's development if recognition by the student of the teacher's qualities leads to veneration or excessive dependence. Nor will close proximity to the teacher help the student approach the teacher's accomplishments. A teacher can do no more than point the way and, sometimes by example, inspire. The work is up to the student. There is no quick or easy way. Finally, it is misguided to expect one's teacher to provide a verbal formula for realizations which cannot be verbalized.

Although a teacher should not foster dependence in his students, he does deserve a full measure of their respect, deference, and loyalty. Students must realize that their teacher is sharing with them the knowledge of an art which he has accumulated over many years of study. If they are to learn what he has to teach, they must trust him and be willing to proceed along the path mapped by him and in the manner he prescribes. Doubts about the teacher's methods are best allayed by reflection on his ability, his years of experience, and on the kind of man he appears to be. If students lack this degree of faith, or refuse to see their role in this light, their continued presence in classes can only be disruptive to their own learning as well as to that of their fellow students.

For best results, our minds should not dwell on the many attractive developments we hope for from our training. Nor should we intellectualize about the presence, or absence, in us of certain abilities said to be characteristic of tai chi masters. Still less should we be concerned with imagining what constitutes these abilities. We must recognize the paramount importance of daily practice, and our mental energies should be fully employed during this practice with doing the form or push-hands as well as we can.

The apparent rate of progress of others in tai chi should not concern or disturb us unless, of course, we are in some way responsible for their development. It is a waste of energy to compare our progress with that of others. If we indulge ourselves in this way, we can always find persons who began their training about the same time as we and who seem to be outdistancing us on the road to some goal we have set. Also, we can easily identify a number of fellow students we seem to have left behind. To base our idea of progress, or our degree of satisfaction with ourselves, on this kind of comparison is fruitless. In calculations of this kind, too many pertinent factors are ignored. The approach which is ultimately most satisfactory is to measure our progress only against ourselves. If we are continuing to move toward living in a more desirable way, we should be content.

A related point concerns the judging of the merits of a system of self-development on the basis of the behavior or other characteristics of adepts in that system. We may reject a system because its chief exponents do not appear to possess those attributes of mind or character the system advertises. On the other hand, we may be drawn to a system because we are attracted by some admirable quality in a person prominent in it. We must also consider the possibility that our experience of life is insufficient to judge their level of development. Nevertheless, this method of evaluation has some validity

173

and should carry some weight. However, we should attach greater importance to an assessment based on actual practice. If the system seems to offer us something, we should give it a try. After practicing for a time (one or two years), we are somewhat better qualified to make a judgment concerning its usefulness for us. In the case of tai chi, we must ask ourselves the following questions: Is tai chi relaxing us? Is it allowing us to open up, to try new things? Is it making our personal relationships easier and more productive? Finally, is it adding to the quality of our life? If the answer to these questions is "Yes," then tai chi has value for us.

The half-hour or more of daily training we undergo should begin to influence us during the rest of our day. The way we sit, stand, walk, and use our body should gradually undergo change, in line with tai chi principles. Our physical and mental health should improve. By giving attention to a tai chi way of moving and thinking throughout our day, we find that we have gradually extended practice far beyond the original formal half-hour. As this process unfolds, we gradually internalize tai chi principles. Only then, can we begin to talk about what has actually happened to us because we can speak from personal experience. In other words, once we set our goal and generally determine the way to get there, all our attention should focus on training. Temptation in the form of imagined or advertised short cuts toward some ephemeral condition of mind or body must be shunned. If we pursue our goal with this mental attitude, progress is guaranteed.

TAI CHI FORM
CONTINUOUS SEQUENCE

Starting Position   1. Preparation   2. Beginning

4. Grasp Bird's Tail (Ward Off with Right Hand)

6. Grasp Bird's Tail (Push)   7. Single Whip

3. Grasp Bird's Tail (Ward Off with Left Hand)

5. Grasp Bird's Tail (Rollback and Press)

8. Lift Hands

9. Shoulder Strike

12. Lift Hands (Left)

13. Brush Knee and Twist
Step (Left)

15. Apparent Closure

 Stork Spreads Wings   11. Brush Knee and Twist Step (Left)

14. Deflect Downward, Parry, and Punch

16. Cross Hands

17. Carry Tiger to Mountain   18. Grasp Bird's Tail (Rollback and Press)

22. Step Back and Repulse Monkey (Right)   23. Step Back and Repulse Monkey (Left)

19. Grasp Bird's Tail (Push)   20. Single Whip

21. Fist Under Elbow

. Step Back and Repulse Monkey (Right)   25. Diagonal Flying

26. Wave Hands Like Clouds (Right)

28. Wave Hands Like Clouds (Right)   29. Single Whip

31. Golden Cock Stands on One Leg (Right)

27. Wave Hands Like Clouds (Left)

30. Snake Creeps Down

2. Golden Cock Stands on One Leg (Left)   33. Separate Right Foot

34. Separate Left Foot

36. Brush Knee and Twist Step (Left)

37. Brush Knee and Twist
Step (Right)

39. Grasp Bird's Tail (Ward Off with Right Hand)

40. Grasp Bird's Ta
(Rollback and Pres

35. Turn and Kick with Heel

38. Step Forward and Punch

41. Grasp Bird's Tail (Push)

42. Single Whip

44. Fair Lady Works at Shuttles (Left)

46. Fair Lady Works at Shuttles (Left)

43. Fair Lady Works at Shuttles (Right)

45. Fair Lady Works at Shuttles (Right)

47. Grasp Bird's Tail (Ward Off with Left Hand)

48. Grasp Bird's Tail (Ward Off with Right Hand)

50. Grasp Bird's Tail (Push)   51. Single Whip

52. Snake Creeps Down   53. Step Forward to Form
Seven Stars

9. Grasp Bird's Tail (Rollback and Press)

54. Retreat to Ride Tiger

55. Turn Around and Kick Horizontally

57. Deflect Downward, Parry, and Punch

58. Apparent Closure

56. Bend Bow and Shoot Tiger

9. Cross Hands

60. Conclusion